NEW MEXICO DEATH RITUALS

A History

ANA PACHECO

THE
History
PRESS

Published by The History Press
Charleston, SC
www.historypress.com

First published 2019

Manufactured in the United States

ISBN 9781467142076

Library of Congress Control Number: 2019948131

Death is not the opposite of life but a part of it.
—Haruki Murakami

CONTENTS

ACKNOWLEDGEMENTS

I would like to express my sincere gratitude to all of the individuals and institutions that so generously gave their time and expertise in assisting me with this book.

In particular, I would like to thank Marcella Sandoval, *Pasa Tiempo*, Hannah Abelbeck, the Palace of the Governors' Photo Archives, Jillian Hartke (digital archivist), Albuquerque Museum, Cindy Abel Morris (photo archivist), the Center for Southwest Research's Special Collections, the University of New Mexico and Patricia Moore at the New Mexico State Library. My heartfelt gratitude also goes out to the longtime residents of Santa Fe, whose memories keep history alive.

This book is dedicated to the contributors of *La Herencia*, who have been my greatest teachers on this journey.

INTRODUCTION

While conducting research for this book, I found that my preoccupation with death is not unique. Death does not discriminate; we're all going to die. The thought of dying gnaws away at us in the shadows of our collective subconscious. Little reminders usually begin with the death of a loved one; then, as we age, the realization of our own death sets in. Today, there's even an app for death. You can download "We Croak" onto your phone, which pings randomly five times a day with the message, "Don't forget, you're going to die." Based on a Buddhist tradition in Bhutan, the app adheres to the belief that the reflection of one's death brings joy in being alive. Since you never know when the ping will occur, it surprises you—just like death.

I had the opportunity to experience the phenomenon of the death process firsthand when I worked at a local funeral home in 2017. My job was to sell pre-need death insurance (a way for people to pay for funeral arrangements in advance). Until then, I never knew that such a thing existed, but I soon found out that it's a big part of the funeral industry. In the 1990s, the funeral industry began to change drastically when the mom-and-pop funeral homes caught the eye of corporate America. Death became very profitable for the living with the consolidation of these small businesses. As competition increased, funeral homes had to appease their stockholders with quarterly profits. Pre-need funeral insurance became an important part of the business model; although the funeral industry couldn't predict when death would occur, funerals were already paid, which added wealth to an already healthy revenue stream. Many major insurance companies began to issue these pre-need policies after funeral homes were caught using the money for other purposes, which left the onus of paying twice for a funeral to the bereaved. Today in New Mexico, the only legal way to sell these policies is through an insurance company. This policy has eased people's minds, because they now know that their money will be held in perpetuity until the person to whom the policy was issued expires.

My brief stint in the industry was with a family-run funeral home, so I was able to experience all aspects of the business. I accompanied the workers on trips to homes and hospitals to pick up the remains of people who had died. I rode with them to take bodies to the crematorium, and I sat in on the embalming process, which is done so families can see their loved ones one last time. During the four and a half months that I worked there, I never found the job to be gruesome or frightening. If anything, I found solace in witnessing the universal passage from life to death.

Setting aside the spiritual concept of an afterlife, this book is meant to highlight the history of death and dying through the eyes of the living. My primary focus is on the early death rituals of Hispanic New Mexico. For two hundred years (from 1610 to 1821), New Mexico was governed by Spain before it became a part of Mexico until 1846. During this era, Catholicism was the only religion practiced in the region. In 1848, when New Mexico became a U.S. territory, the state's cultural death rituals slowly evolved to include more Protestant traditions, as well as those of other faiths.

This book would not be complete if it didn't include a chapter on Día de los Muertos. Some might wonder why it's not the lead chapter, but that tradition did not come to New Mexico until much later. Even when New Mexico was a part of Mexico (from 1821 to 1846) the celebration of the Day of the Dead was not widespread. It wasn't until the latter part of the twentieth century, when an influx of Mexican immigrants began to arrive, that the popularity of Día de los Muertos gained momentum in the state.

The unrelenting pace of life in the twenty-first century has accelerated the Hispanic tradition of death rituals in New Mexico. Traditionally, funerals were three-day events: the first day was reserved for visitation with the dead; on the evening of the second day, a communal rosary was held with the deceased and their family present; and on the last day, a funeral mass was held, followed by a celebration of life. Today, many families are spread out in distant cities and have busy work schedules that don't allow for the lengthy funeral process. It has become more common for the visitation, rosary, funeral and reception to be held on the same day so that people can get back to the business of life.

Now, when people come to town to visit their departed loved ones, they have access to a convenient grave-finder app. New Mexicans have been quick to adopt some of the more popular modern death rituals such as cremation, green burials and contributions to science through body donation. In the neighboring state of Colorado, the only sanctioned open-air pyre in the United States is operated in Crestone and provides an alternative to normal cremation techniques. The Maxwell Museum at the University of New Mexico in Albuquerque has the largest contemporary collection of human bones in the world. The museum allows families to visit the bones of their loved ones who now reside in their repository.

One Hispanic death ritual in New Mexico that has gone unchanged is the *descanso* (the roadside memorial described in the second chapter of this book). Not only have these public shrines grown to include other cultures, their popularity has spread throughout the country. The proliferation of these makeshift tributes has created such controversy that many states have enacted laws that either protect or condemn these remembrances to the dead.

Along with the expedited funeral, New Mexico has become part of the growing trend of "death tourism" in the state. Around the globe, historic places associated with death and tragedy have historically been touted as destination trips. Tourists want to experience the dark history of the mummies in Guanajuato, Mexico; the catacombs in Paris; the genocide museum in Rwanda; and the tombs of ancient Egypt. Two of the most widely visited sites in New Mexico are the graves of Smokey Bear in the Capitan Mountains and Billy the Kid's grave at Fort Sumner. Also located at Fort Sumner is the Bosque Redondo Memorial, which was created in 2005 to remember the hundreds of Mescalero Apache and Navajo Indians who died there between 1864 and 1868 under the "auspices" of the U.S. government. Coincidentally, the Bosque Redondo Memorial is located on Billy the Kid Road.

Native American death rituals are not widely included in this book with the exception of those that are similar to Catholic funeral practices. Beginning in the late 1800s and through the following century, the study of Native peoples included the disinterment of burial grounds, which caused turmoil for living tribal members, as it was considered a sign of disrespect for their ancestors. The human remains and artifacts found at these burial grounds often ended up as museum exhibitions. In 1990, the Native American Graves Protection and Repatriation Act (NAGPRA) took effect and provided protection for indigenous people on the issue of archaeological mortuary studies both past and current. NAGPRA also monitors projects and museum collections as they relate to human remains.

A significant part of my research comes from the work of several contributors to *La Herencia* (The Heritage), the quarterly magazine I published from 1994 to 2009. As I went through the back issues, I discovered that there were multiple articles pertaining to death in many of them. Ironically, most of these contributors have since passed away, but their legacy continues with this book.

This book is not meant to depress the reader; rather, like the "We Croak" app, it's my hope that it'll serve as a reminder that we're all going to die. In the meantime, enjoy the ride!

1
DEATH'S CULTURAL CONNECTION

Since the beginning of time, two facts of life have remained constant: people just can't seem to get along with each other and everyone has a fear of death. The circumstances of historical discord vary, but the fear of death that is woven into our collective consciousness is universal. Unable to grasp life's finality, people have always turned to a belief in an afterlife in order to grapple with the unknown. Virtually every culture in the world adheres to the notion that a new life begins when our current one ceases to exist. Throughout the world, the ritual of death continues to navigate the journey beyond, and as in life, these rituals are dictated by social mores.

The Wadi Al-Salem Cemetery is the largest cemetery in the world, covering 1,485.5 acres, which is about 2.3 square miles. Approximately five million bodies are buried in the cemetery located in Najaf, Iraq. Muslims believe that Wadi Al-Salem, which means Valley of Peace in Arabic, is a part of heaven, and it is there that they wish to be buried. Iraq is located between the Tigris and Euphrates Rivers in the area known as Mesopotamia. Referred to as the cradle of civilization, this region grew to include other countries in the Near and Middle East. At Wadi Al-Salem, nobles are entombed in structures high above ground so that people in the neighboring communities can be reminded of their status in life. Members of the hierarchy also built deep underground full-sized rooms for the dead that were only accessible by ladders. Since its inception in 1400, every social class, from sultans to paupers, has found peace at Wadi Al-Salem.

In neighboring Egypt, grandiose burial chambers continue to be unearthed, revealing the treasures of the ancient pharaohs that have provided the narrative of that ancient civilization. Even more fantastical than the riches that are discovered is the process of mummification that the Egyptians mastered through trial and error around 2600 BC. They believed that a person's soul would not remain intact as the body decayed, so they created a process that stopped the body from deteriorating. First, the brain was extracted through the nostrils with an iron hook, then they removed the internal organs and washed them in a mixture of palm wine and spices before placing them in ornate jars made of limestone. The heart remained in the body, since it was considered the center of intelligence. Natron, a mixture of sodium carbonate and sodium bicarbonate (salt and baking soda) that was plentiful along the dry riverbeds, was the main ingredient used to dry out the body. They would cover the body with the dehydrating agent before placing it in a linen body bag for up to forty days to draw out moisture and preserve the skin and muscle tissues.

While Egyptian mummies are the most well-known preserved bodies, the preservation of the dead actually started on the other side of the planet in South America in 4000 BC. In the northern coastal region of what is now present-day Chile, the Paloma tribe mummified their dead using salt and other dehydrating agents. The bodies were positioned with their knees close to their chests and their hands clasped prior to being buried underneath the family home. A thousand years later, the Chinchoros tribe, also in Chile, used their own process that began by dissembling the corpse and removing the organs. Once the body was emptied of its internal organs, the body was put back together using wood to support the spine, legs and arms. The body was then filled with feathers and covered in clay, which was sculpted to depict the face of a person. These death masks gave the spirit an enduring physical form and were adopted by different cultures around the world. The Incan civilization of Peru carried on the ritual of mummification until Spanish colonization in the 1600s. The arid climate in Peru dried the bodies naturally, which were arranged in a fetal position, wrapped in leather or cloth and placed in baskets or ceramic jars. The Paracas mummy of Peru was entombed in layers of rich fabric in the belief that wearing wealth would buy status in the next world.

The concept of attaining a higher position in the afterlife through wealth was a common practice throughout ancient civilization, but it was during the thirteenth century that the Catholic Church began the practice of "paying the way" to a new level. In 1245, Pope Innocent IV needed funds to complete the construction of Westminster Abbey in London, so he told his congregants that they would be able to spend less time in Purgatory if they donated money. That was the beginning of the practice of paying for masses for the dead in order to hasten the time their souls have to spend waiting to get into Heaven, which is a tradition that continues today. In the sixteenth century, a German monk by the name of Martin Luther took a defiant stance with the contention that the Roman Catholic Church was corrupt. What drew his considerable ire was the claim that church donations would limit the amount of time an individual would spend in Purgatory. His distrust of the Catholic hierarchy led to the founding of the Lutheran Church.

All religions address the concept of the afterlife differently. The Hindu, Buddhist and Jainism faiths all believe in reincarnation or the belief that once a person dies, their soul leaves to become another living organism resulting in karma, or fate, based on the actions they practiced in life. Those who lived a good life would be reborn to a higher realm. The Hindu believe that death doesn't take place until the skull is split open by the extreme heat of a pyre. In Judaism, it is said that souls take flight at the moment of death and the body becomes a vessel of that transition. In some parts of the world, birds have played an integral part in death rituals and the journey of the soul. In the harsh climate of Tibet, sky burials are performed; the bodies of the dead are left on large rock slabs above the frozen ground, where they are reduced to bones by scavenging birds. Both the Lakota Sioux in the United States and the Aboriginal people of Australia place bodies on tree platforms, where they can be picked clean by birds. In Iran, death's transition takes place at the Towers of Silence, where crows and vultures eat the flesh of the dead while the body is in a state of limbo. Also known as *dahkma*, these raised circular structures are used in the funerary ritual of the Zoroastrians. This Persian faith adheres to the belief that the four elements—fire, water, earth and air—are sacred and that to dispose of the dead in any other manner than at the Towers of Silence would pollute the earth. A platform is built at the top of the towers, where the bodies of men are placed on an outer circle, women are placed in the middle and children are placed in an inner circle. When there are enough vultures in the area, the stripping of the flesh from a body can occur in a matter of thirty minutes.

Since the beginning of civilization, diverse cultures have all believed that in death, an individual was deserving of the same social status they enjoyed in life. In 200 BC, Shi Huangdi, China's first emperor, was buried with a terra-cotta army of five thousand life-sized ceramic soldiers that were to

Above: A covered body in Kathmandu, Nepal, waits to be taken to the Pashupatinath Temple as part of the Hindu ritual prior to cremation. *Photograph by Ana Pacheco.*

Opposite, top: The cremation of the dead at Pashupatinath Temple in Kathmandu, Nepal. *Photograph by Ana Pacheco.*

Opposite, bottom: A worker collects cremated remains to be spread in the Bagmati River, which is located next to the Pashupatinath Temple. In the Hindu religion, the Bagmati River is sacred because it flows into the Ganges River in India. *Photograph by Ana Pacheco.*

defend him in the afterlife. The Egyptian pharaohs and other heads of nobility around the globe were interred with the riches they had amassed while living. Even those of lesser means would take their special possessions with them. In the belief that death is but a voyage to another life, chariots, wagons and other forms of transportation were buried with the dead. The Vikings couldn't bury their ships, so instead, they created ship motifs above their graves. In the Arctic region of Siberia, nomadic peoples would sacrifice a prized reindeer to honor the dead. The Lakota Sioux tribe shared a similar tradition in which they would kill the horse of a fallen warrior so it could carry him to the land of the dead.

In addition to the ritual of burying the dead with their prized possessions, grieving families often aid their deceased loved ones by providing them with

material goods. The Inuit of Alaska dress the dead in parkas, boots and mittens to keep them warm on their journey. In the Czech Republic, the dead are buried with boots for their hike to the next world. Chinese mourners take toiletries to the grave so the dead can freshen up. In Madagascar, radios are left at gravesites so the deceased can be entertained and catch up on the latest news. Burial with food at the gravesites is another worldwide phenomenon, and it is done to provide sustenance for the dead as they travel to the afterlife.

Like food, some cultures also believed that sex had an important connection to death. In Sumatra, the Karo Batak believed that if a young boy and girl died unexpectedly, they missed one of the important stages of life. During their funeral, a ritual marriage would be performed so that they could fulfill their destiny. The boy's penis would be enclosed in a piece of bamboo and the girl would be penetrated with a banana to consummate the union. Other cultures viewed death as another stage of life, just like birth. The concept of "womb to tomb" is practiced in many cultures. In Southeast Asia, the entrances of tombs are designed to resemble a vagina beneath a mound of earth. Through the ages, sex, like death, was on everybody's mind. In the sixteenth century the Elizabethan poet John Donne wrote a poem in which he used the word "die" in place of "orgasm" to describe carnal ecstasy. In France, it was not uncommon to hear the phrase *petite mort* (the little death) when describing an orgasm. Even Sigmund Freud, the founder of psychoanalysis, likened sexual pleasure with death. His observation was influenced by Greek mythology when he concluded that Eros, the god of love, and Thanatos, the god of death, were intrinsically linked. He theorized that through sex, people sought to escape the tensions of life if only for a few blissful moments, just as he imagined it would be at the moment of death.

Belief in an afterlife doesn't necessarily ease the fear of death, so many cultures choose to mock death instead. From the drunken Irish wake, to the Day of the Dead celebrations in Mexico and Halloween in the United States, many traditions surrounding death began as a way of banishing thoughts of the unknown while having a jolly good time in the process. The merriment extended to the genre of the humorous epitaphs that began in England at the beginning of the eighteenth century and later included comic verses being etched onto tombstones.

The belief that women bring life into the world and should, therefore, guide it to the end is universal. Not only were women expected to bathe and dress the corpse, but they were also expected to make preparations for the funeral and cook for the mourners attending the death ceremony. In Ireland and the Middle East, women were expected to lament in sorrow for the dead by keening and reciting dirges. During the fourteenth century in India, the practice known as *sati*, a Sanskrit term that means "the woman chooses the right path," was practiced; in absolute devotion to their husbands, wives would jump into the flames of their husbands' pyre. It was seen as a culminating moment for couples, as they were set aflame dressed in their wedding outfits. As the woman's shrieks of horror and pain grew louder, members of the funeral party added wood to the fire, not only to hasten the woman's anguish but also to keep her from escaping the flames. The practice of *sati* continued in some parts of India throughout the nineteenth century. In a show of absolute fidelity to their husbands, women in Borneo were expected to stay in a small dark room with the decomposing body for eleven days, eating just enough to provide minimal sustenance while sharing food with their dead husbands. That mourning practice continued through the latter part of the twentieth century.

Throughout history, faith has guided humanity on a righteous path in the hope of something better after death, but there is one group for which death holds no future. Atheism, the lack of belief in a god, can be traced back to ancient Greece. During the fifth century, Diagoras of Melos, considered the father of atheism, was condemned to death for being a godless person and narrowly escaped execution. Socrates, however, wasn't so lucky. In 399 BC, he was sentenced to death for not believing in the gods of the state and for corrupting the minds of youth with his teachings. Rather than accede to the demands of the government, Socrates chose to drink his punishment of poisonous hemlock. For the Greek philosopher, living a life unexamined was more frightening than the possibility of damnation in the afterlife.

2
DEATH MARKERS

The roadside crosses found along New Mexico byways and highways mark the spots where lives have ended tragically. The practice of placing crosses and stones to create devotional homages to the deceased is practiced by cultures around the world. With the increase of random acts of violence filling the nightly news, this ritual has morphed into a universal tradition, spontaneously marking the spot as a memorial with flowers, photos and candles for the dead.

In New Mexico, these death markers are known as *descansos*, which is derived from the Spanish word *decansar* (to rest). The tradition of the *descanso* began with the sixteenth-century confraternity La Fraternidad Piadosa de Nuestro Padre Jesus Nazareno, which is also known as Los Hermanos Penitentes (the Brotherhood of the Repentant). The Penitentes placed crosses or laid stones to mark the places of their fellow Spaniards' deaths along El Camino Real de Tierra Adentro (Camino Real). These remembrances were erected for the colonists who died from exposure or were killed by Natives along the treacherous 1,500-mile trade route that began in Mexico City and ended in San Gabriel in northern New Mexico. The *descanso* was a memorial for the *anima* (soul) of the deceased. Las Cruces, the state's largest city to the south, got its name from the crosses that were erected along that trail for the dead.

During Holy Week, the Penitentes visit the different *moradas* (meetinghouses), marking the ground with stones and crosses as a form of a *descanso*. They periodically stop to pray and rest at these marked locations

In 1847, crosses were etched in a petrographic style on this rock in northern New Mexico to signify the Spanish and Native American lives lost during the beginning of the American occupation. *Courtesy of* La Herencia *Photo Archives.*

as they carry the *maderos* (large crosses). Christianity is universally identified by the cross, which in Spanish is called *cruz*, a word derived from the Latin word *crux* that means an upright post crossed by a lateral piece of wood. Place names throughout New Mexico are named for the cross, including Las Cruces in Doña Ana County, Santa Cruz in Río Arriba County, Camino de Cruz Blanca in Santa Fe County and Santa Cruz Lake in Los Alamos County. New Mexican artisans promote the cross in their art, which often includes freestanding wooden crosses. In the capital city of Santa Fe, north of the town square plaza, the Cross of the Martyrs sits on a hillside above the city as a reminder of the twenty-one Franciscan priests who died during the 1680 Pueblo Revolt. This cross, made of steel, is painted white and has a panoramic view of Santa Fe.

Like the olive trees that cover the hills of southern Spain, *descansos* dot the landscape of New Mexico. Glimpses of these memorials act as a warning to motorists zooming down the highway: slow down or become the next traffic fatality. Roadside memorials are all different, just like the people they commemorate. Some are more elaborate than others; along with the requisite cross, they're often adorned with flowers, images of saints, photos and personal items that best describe the personality of the deceased. There

Cross and rock *descansos* from 1935 in Truchas, New Mexico. *Photo by T. Harman Parkhurst. Courtesy of Palace of the Governors [NMHM/DCA]. No. 011591.*

are also less ornate, simple white crosses. A cluster of crucifixes indicates that several people, perhaps an entire family, lost their lives in that locale. Shards of scattered glass shimmering like specks of mica in stone, along with rubber skid marks, introduce a newly formed *descanso*. As time passes, the *descanso* begins to evolve. Family and friends continue to decorate them for different holidays; *descansos* will sometimes be decorated with Christmas wreaths, birthday balloons and Valentine's Day hearts. Theses memorials are not gravesites; rather, they are collages of love and devotion erected by the side of the road. The *descanso* marks the spot of the tragic end of a life. Some may have died immediately at the location, while others may have passed on the way to the hospital.

Roadside memorials have become such a ubiquitous part of the American landscape that the Spanish term *descansos* is used in other parts of the country, but these homages to the dead are not appreciated by all. The State of New Jersey allows people to create a memorial on the Atlantic City Expressway but only with the assistance of a police escort, and they can

A *descanso* used as a marker by the Hermanos Penitentes to mark the path to the *morada*. *Courtesy of* La Herencia *Photo Archives.*

Left: Plastic flowers with a cross symbolize the Catholic rosary on a *descanso* near Velarde, New Mexico. *Courtesy of* La Herencia *Photo Archives.*

Below: Three crosses erected by the Hermanos Penitentes during Holy Week. *Courtesy of* La Herencia *Photo Archives.*

A tilted wooden cross at a *camposanto* in northern New Mexico in 1975. *Photograph by David Donoho. Courtesy of the Palace of the Governors [NMHM/DCA]. No. 157660.*

only be up for ten days after the accident has occurred. Texas only allows roadside memorials if the motorist was killed as a result of a DUI accident. In Colorado, the state's chapter of the ACLU protested the placement of wooden crosses, citing the separation of church and state. After the public in Colorado expressed outrage over the ban, officials tried to quell the controversy by placing rectangular blue signs at accident sites; however, the memorials are not permanent, and they are removed after two years by the highway department. Both Florida and Wisconsin ban the practice of roadside memorials altogether, citing safety issues for the motorists who may be distracted by the memorials and for those creating memorials on busy

Left: Artificial roses cover this metal cross *descanso* with a rock image of Our Lady of Guadalupe at the bottom. *Photograph by Ana Pacheco.*

Below: A statue of Our Lady of Guadalupe erected at the site of a *descanso* with plastic flowers at the pedestal. *Photograph by Ana Pacheco.*

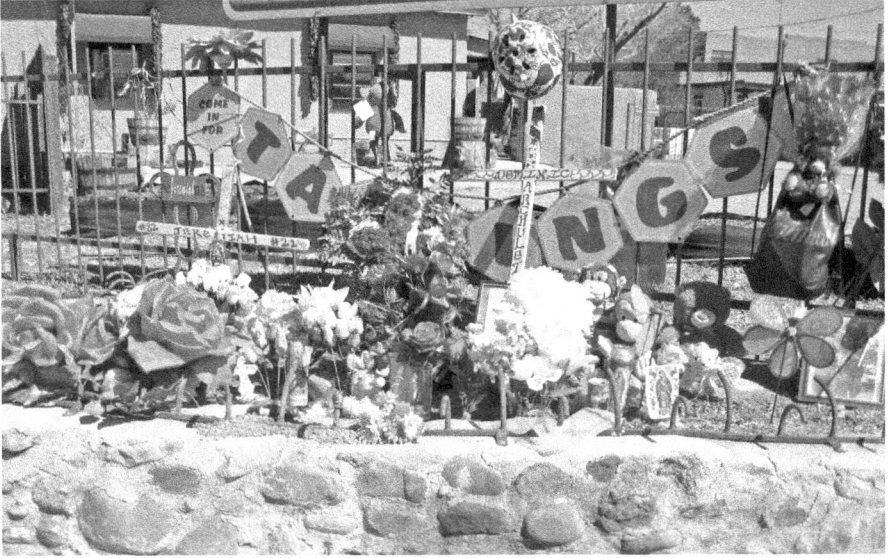

In the early part of 2019, a father and son were killed in front of this business at the corner of Paseo de Peralta and St. Francis Drive in Santa Fe. Within a few days, a *descanso* was created as a memorial for the tragic loss. *Photograph by Ana Pacheco.*

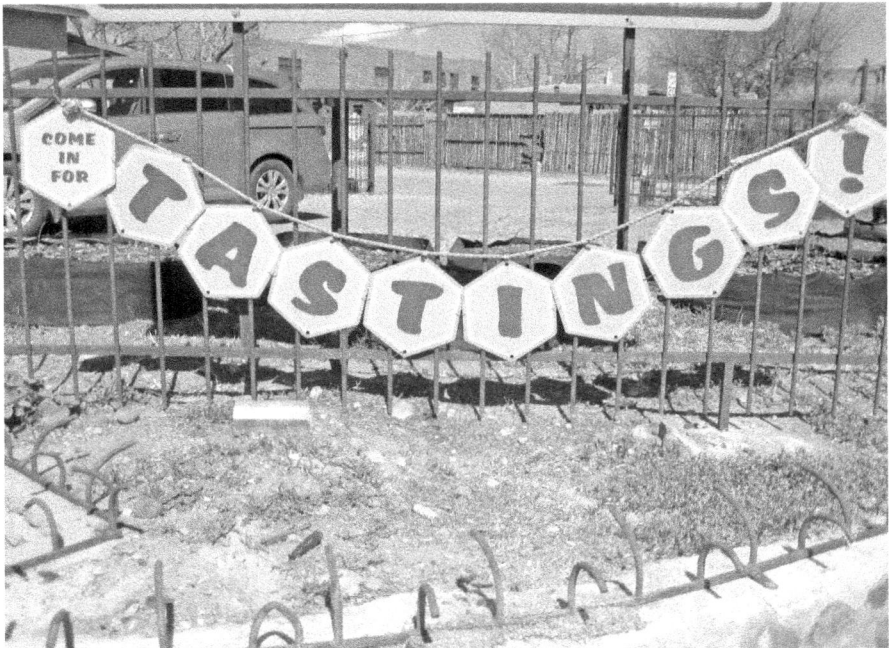

The owner of the business allowed for the creation of the *descanso* to remain in front of the business for a month following the accident before removing it. *Photograph by Ana Pacheco.*

This *descanso* indicates that two people lost their lives in this location. *Photograph by Ana Pacheco.*

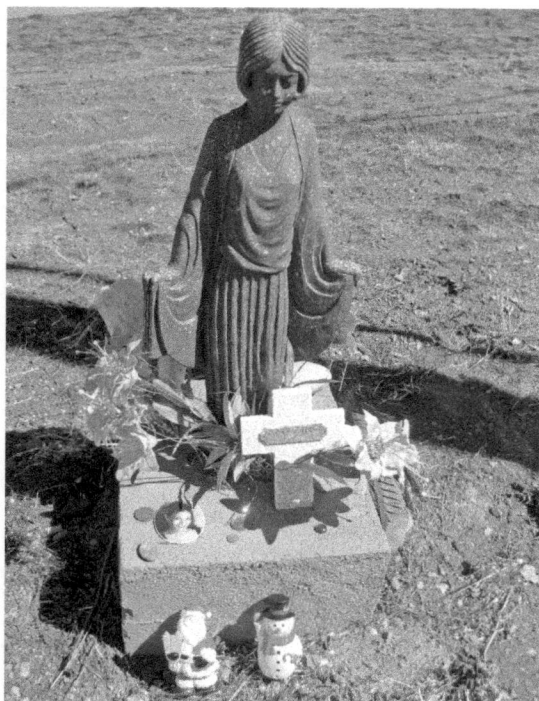

A statue was erected as a *descanso* at the location of an automobile accident to honor a young woman who was killed. *Photograph by Ana Pacheco.*

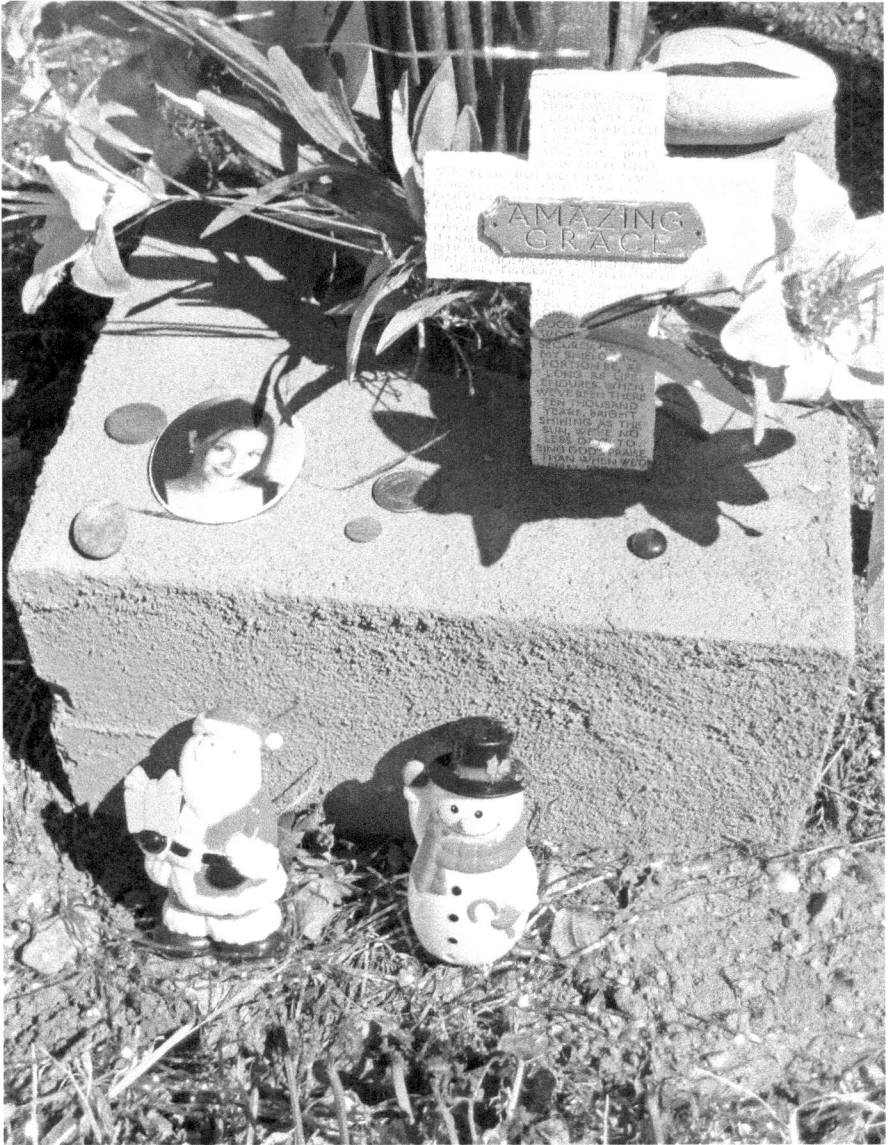

A photograph of the young woman, a plastic Santa Claus and snowman and an Alcoholics Anonymous sobriety medallion are at the pedestal of the statue. The medallion indicates that alcohol may have been involved in the fatal car accident. *Photograph by Ana Pacheco.*

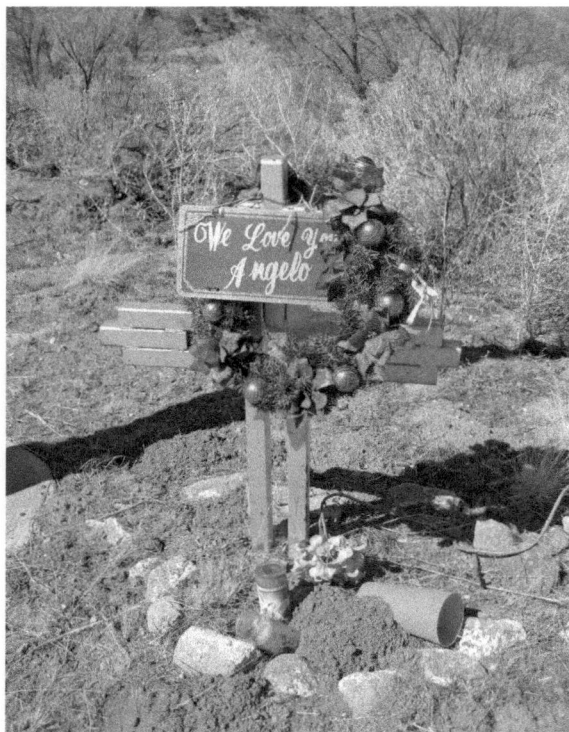

A Christmas wreath and a sign reading, "We Love You Angelo," is placed over the metal cross *descanso*. *Photograph by Ana Pacheco.*

highways. Safety concerns are a valid consideration for these memorials, but the religious connotation of their placement on public roadways is the underlying objection to this type of memorial. The Wisconsin-based group Freedom from Religion objects to the memorial crosses and has demanded that they be removed throughout the country.

At the epicenter of this four-hundred-year-old tradition, New Mexico's roadside memorials are not only woven into the state's cultural fabric, but they have also become a part of its legislation. In 2007, the New Mexico state legislature passed a law that states, "*Descansos* are a memorial, placed alongside a public road right of way to memorialize the death of one or more persons. It is illegal to remove or desecrate a *Descanso*." In the event that roadside work is needed in an area where one of these roadside memorials has been erected, the highway department must carefully remove the *descanso* and replace it once the work is completed. In recent years, a new genre of the roadside memorial in New Mexico has become sacrosanct: ghost bikes. The increase in bicyclists on the road has led to the deaths of several people by motorists, and ghost bikes are dedicated remembrances to them. Unlike

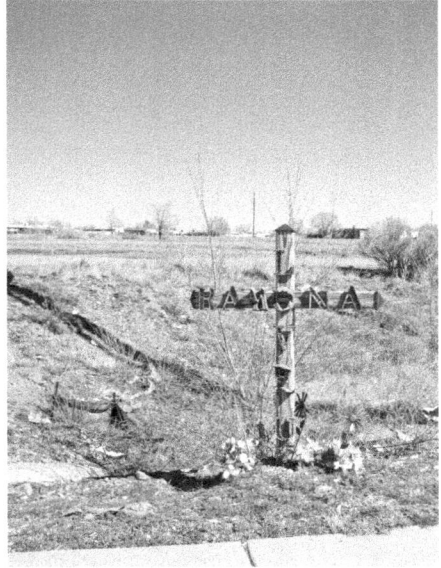

Left: The site of a *descanso* under a "Do Not Enter" sign that went unnoticed by the motorist who was killed while entering the wrong side of the road. *Photograph by Ana Pacheco.*

Right: A *descanso* featuring a wooden cross with the name "Ramona" carved into it. *Photograph by Ana Pacheco.*

Flowers adorn this *descanso* placed between two rocks with the initials "GR" at the center of the cross. *Photograph by Ana Pacheco.*

In New Mexico, tributes to bicyclists killed on the road are called "ghost bike" memorials. Like the *descanso*, personal mementos are left at the site, while the name of the deceased is etched on the bike rather than a cross. *Photograph by Ana Pacheco.*

the traditional *descanso*, which is usually a few feet from the ground, ghost bikes feature full-frame white replicas of bicycles, making them highly visible on the highway. The memorials have information about the deceased along with personal objects that adorn the bikes' frames. The Albuquerque city council also passed legislation for this type of *descanso*, making it illegal to desecrate, deface, destroy or remove ghost bikes.

3
THE LIFE OF DEATH

Embalming, the ancient practice refined by the Egyptians (circa 1550–1069 BC), was readily available in Europe and the big cities of the American Northeast during the mid-nineteenth century. It wasn't until the American Civil War (1861–65), however, that the culture of death in the United States was transformed with the expanded use of embalming. More than half a million soldiers died on the battlefields hundreds of miles away from their grieving families, who all wanted to bring their loved ones back home for burial and were willing to pay to have them put in a state of preservation. It was a pivotal moment in our nation's history that cultivated our handling of the dead into a regulated, mainstream industry. Although the science of embalming was available in Albuquerque and Santa Fe as early as 1848, for most Hispanic communities through the mid-1940s, the preparation and the burial of a loved one was the responsibility of the family. In the event that the deceased had no family, or if they did not live in close proximity to their family members, the task of caring for the remains was left to the community.

Church bells would ring throughout the small villages and towns in New Mexico to alert the community of the death of one of its members. Men were assigned the task of ringing the bells, which tolled in sequence: nine times for a man, six for a woman and three for a child. If an infant had died, the bells would not toll but ring out joyously to celebrate the belief that the child had been baptized in their first eight months of life and, therefore, was automatically granted eternal life in heaven. Leaflets would also be printed to announce deaths and keep towns informed, since most villages lacked telephones and daily newspapers. These death notices were given to family members, friends, neighbors and church parishioners. The U.S. Postal Service handled the distribution of the death announcements to relatives in far-off places.

As the men took care of the various modes of communication, the women were given the more important task of caring for the remains of the dead. This part of the death ritual stemmed from the belief that women were the ones who brought life into the world, and therefore, it seemed only natural that they also brought life to its end. The ritual of bathing and dressing the body and organizing the wake were conducted in the homes of the deceased. Vinegar was used in the bathing process as a form of preservation. It was customary for older family members to choose their burial clothing in order to ease the burden of their loved ones at the time of their deaths. In many of the isolated villages, electricity was either sparse or nonexistent, so expediency in caring for the dead was of utmost importance to minimize the decaying process. It was also customary for the men to build the coffin, rearrange the furniture in the house to accommodate the casket in preparation for the wake, cut wood to heat the house and dig the grave. Other women in the community, who were not involved in the preparation of the body, would return to their homes to prepare food for the *dolientes* (mourners), who would stop by to pay their respects. The most common food made for these occasions was an abundant array of chile dishes. During this era, the colloquialism *"Chilorio Velorio"* (chile wake) was borne into the vernacular of northern New Mexico.

Once preparations were completed, usually by the next day, people gathered at a given hour for the *velorio* (wake). A *rezador* (cantor) led the mourners in prayer, and it was later accompanied by *alabados* (sacred hymns). The wake began with lamenting and loud wailing followed by silent meditation and praying the rosary. Once the ceremony was completed, people would gather to eat the prepared food before leaving to prepare for the funeral the next morning.

Family members sat vigil with the body through the night not only in remorse but also in the belief that the person's soul remained and that their prayers would help their *anima* (soul) reach a higher attainment. The nightly vigil not only had a spiritual connotation but also stemmed from an earlier belief that death did not occur at a single moment. Long before the advent of stethoscopes, which are used to detect heartbeats, dead bodies would be pricked with needles to see if there was any response. The living would sit with the deceased through the night to make sure there were no signs of life, so they would be assured that their loved one would not be buried alive. During the heyday of trade along the Santa Fe Trail, a merchant by the name of Antonio Otero experienced the unthinkable. While away in Missouri securing a caravan of goods, his wife died and was buried. When Otero returned, he was filled with remorse and wanted to see her one last time, so he had her body exhumed. When the coffin was opened, her clothes were torn and some of her hair had been pulled out in a futile attempt to escape the underground chamber. Apparently, the woman had gone into a coma but had not died. To the horror of the family and community, the wife of Antonio Otero had been buried alive.

The Native Americans held a similar custom of staying with the deceased through the night. Most tribes believed that when a person died, they began a four-day journey to the spirit world. As the body began to decompose, their memory would live on through their descendants. During this period of mourning, loved ones would come to accept that life was a cycle that reached its conclusion at the time of death.

After the nightly vigil, bodies would be taken by wagon or truck to the church for a funeral mass. When the deceased arrived, the pallbearers would carry the casket into the church, where it was met by the priest who performed a special prayer and blessed the casket with holy water. The casket was then led to the altar, where it would remain through the mass. After the service, the pallbearers, led by the priest, would carry the casket on their shoulders to the cemetery, which was usually outside of the church perimeter. After the blessing of the grave, special prayers would be recited by the priest, as the coffin was lowered into the grave with ropes. Each of the mourners would toss a handful of dirt into the grave as it was being covered by the men of the community.

After the funeral, everyone would return to the home of the deceased, where they

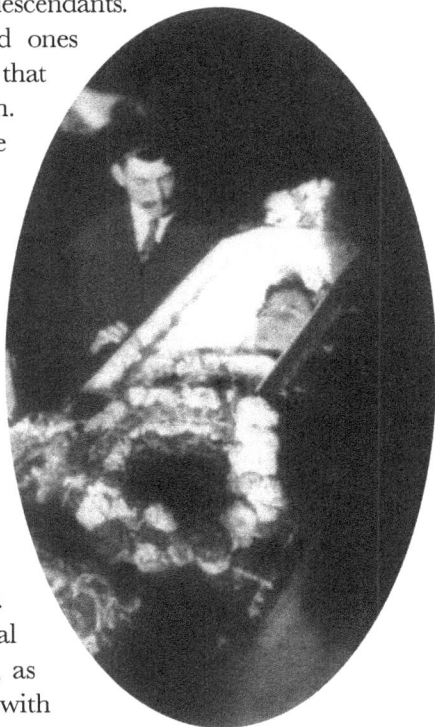

Family members would sit vigil with the deceased through the night praying that the soul of the departed would ascend to heaven. *Courtesy* La Herencia *Photo Archives.*

Native Americans also shared in the belief of remaining with a lost loved one while their spirit ascended to a higher realm. *Warren E. Rollins, Grief, 1917, oil on canvas, forty-four by sixty-six inches. Collection of the New Mexico Museum of Art. Photo by Cameron Gray.*

would be greeted by the women who stayed to prepare the food. They would also return the furniture in the house, which had been cleared away for the casket, to its regular format. Community members would stay after the reception to help the bereaved complete the funeral process, which included making the headstone for the grave. Commercially made headstones were sparse or unaffordable, so it was up to the locals to make them with whatever type of rock was plentiful and easy to carve, like flagstone.

Once the funeral was over, the ritual of paying for special masses for the dead began. The eight-day mass came first, followed by a thirty-day mass and, then, as many masses as people could afford to pay to the church throughout the year. There was a strong belief held at that time that the more masses offered for the deceased, the better chance that he or she would gain eternal life in heaven. The one-year anniversary mass was almost as important as the actual funeral mass, with people gathering at the home of the deceased once again to mourn with the bereaved and to partake in another banquet of chile dishes.

The constant reminder of death in the community was emphasized through fashion. The *tápalo* (black shawl) was the requisite garment for women, and it was to be worn for a full year after the passing of a loved one. This symbol of mourning was widely worn by New Mexican women from the 1600s to the mid-1900s. The vertical garment covered the body from head to ankle; it was yet another vestige that had been woven into the culture after several centuries of Moorish occupation in Spain that eventually trickled down to the distant settlements of the empire. The *tápalo* is reminiscent of the hijab and burka worn by women in the Muslim world today. During this era in New Mexico, the *tápalo* was such an important part of a person's legacy that it was often listed in a person's will to be handed down to the next woman in the family. It was also often presented as a wedding gift by the groom to the bride so that she could wear the *tápalo* at the time of his death. These black shawls were also worn by other women in the community when they went to express *el pésame* (condolences) to those who had lost a loved one. As these women donned their mourning attire, they paid their respects with the traditional protocol, which included an emotional display by the widow that included weeping and wailing endearing remembrances for the deceased that were known as a *requiebro* (to lament the memory of the dead). The *requiebro* is also attributed to the Moorish custom of reciting dirges for the dead. The typical *requiebro* by a widow included:

> *Ya tofuiste y me dejaste sola. ¿Que voy a hacer sin tí vida mía? Se nublara mi casa enternamente.*

> *My house will be forevermore without light. What will I do without you, My Beloved? You've left me alone and desolate.*

The black shawl, known as the *tápalo*, was a symbol of mourning widely worn by women in New Mexico from the 1600s to the mid-twentieth century. *Photo John S. Candelario. Courtesy of the Palace of the Governors [NMHM/DCA]. No. 0165857.*

Above: A mourning shroud was often presented by a groom to his bride on their wedding day. Widows were required to wear the *tápalo* for one year after their husbands' deaths. *Courtesy* La Herencia *Photo Archives.*

Left: The vertical garment covered the body from head to ankle and was a vestige of the Moorish culture that had been woven into Spanish traditions even in the distant settlements of the Spanish empire. *Courtesy* La Herencia *Photo Archives.*

Women wore the *tápolo* when they went to pay their respects to the bereaved and on visits to the cemetery. *Courtesy of the Palace of the Governors [NMHM/DCA]. No. 058598.*

A deluge of settlers descended from the east when New Mexico became a U.S. territory in 1848, and by the end of the century, they had transformed the culture of the small towns and villages. Longtime residents felt that there was a need to preserve the Spanish cultural traditions of their ancestors, especially the ritual of death. During this era, groups of men in northern New Mexico and southern Colorado founded organizations that evolved into tightly linked networks of people to promote the culture and help people suffering from illness, financial hardship and the death of a family member. These societies helped the bereaved by providing resources to bury their loved ones with honor, including the ancestral tradition of praying the rosary and singing *alabados* in Spanish. In 1916, Marcelino Apodaca founded La Union Protectiva De Santa Fe (LUPDSF) in Santa Fe. Today, LUPDSF continues with the women's branch of the organization, La Union Protectiva Feminina, regularly conducting fundraisers and annual meetings to raise money for members' funerals and praying the rosary at the time of death.

As the Anglo population continued to grow, funeral practices began to change in New Mexico's larger towns. Funeral goods such as coffins and headstones were starting to be transported from the east on the Santa Fe Trail. Funeral homes were established and offered the science of embalming as a way to preserve a loved one for a final visit with their

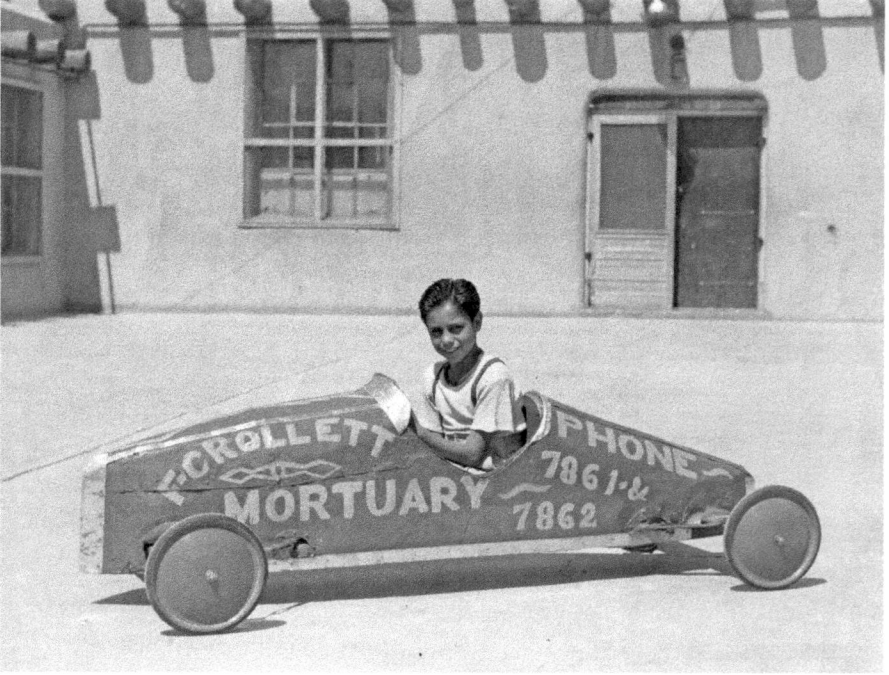

During the twentieth century, the funeral industry marketed its services in unique ways in some of New Mexico's largest towns. *Courtesy* La Herencia *Photo Archives.*

family members. The tradition of caring for the dead at home fell out of fashion with these new businesses taking over all aspects of the funeral process. Advertisements in Spanish promoting undertaker services began to appear in daily newspapers. By the mid-twentieth century, the funeral industry was well established through aggressive marketing tactics that conveyed the idea that caring for the dead was an unseemly task best left to professionals.

4
RIP

The tradition of subterranean church interment that was followed in Spain and Mexico was also followed in New Mexico during the seventeenth and eighteenth centuries. Wealthy parishioners, as well as members of the *cofradias* (confraternities), received the prime burial locations beneath churches throughout the state. The wealthy often paid extra to be placed near the altar or next to the statue of a saint. Special care was given to ensure that the cadavers' heads were positioned toward the east, since it was believed that Christ's resurrection would come from that direction. The families of the deceased also believed that if their loved ones were buried below the altar of sacred relics, or near a statue of a saint, they would receive special benefits in heaven. They also believed that the prayers of the living during church services would intercede on behalf of the souls of the dead. These underground church cemeteries were a constant reminder for the living to continue on a pious path, because one day, they would join their dead brethren below. These underground burials did not include the use of a coffin; the remains were wrapped in cloth and were free of any type of valuables to discourage grave robbing. During this period, the Spanish mandate stated that a burial plot was to be used multiple times; following a three-year time period, allowing for the process of decay, the newly deceased were buried with the bones of others. Due to the high rate of infant mortality, the church could not accommodate each burial, so babies were often buried beneath the family home. Throughout the twentieth century, the bones of infants were often discovered during the remodeling of old homes in northern

New Mexico. When the bones of these infants were discovered, they were returned to the family for a proper burial. Hispanics referred to their dead babies as *angelitos* (little angels) in the belief that since they died before the age of reasoning, they were immediately reunited with their creator.

During outbreaks of smallpox and other epidemics, the dead were buried in mass graves far from the church to avoid contagion. These communal graves were also used during Native raids that resulted in numerous fatalities. Since it was commonly believed that burial within close proximity of the church provided a gateway for the soul, the bones of a loved were often retrieved at a later date for a proper burial on sacred ground.

Often, even the remains of those who died far from home were brought back for a proper burial. In the 1830s, Manuel Salustiano Delgado, an enterprising businessman, contracted cholera and died along the Santa Fe Trail en route from Franklin, Missouri. His death occurred during the summer hundreds of miles from New Mexico. The people on the wagon train knew that because of the heat and distance, his remains would not make it back for a proper burial. One of their Native guides, Susano Leyba, was very knowledgeable about the terrain and chose a familiar site for his burial. Delgado's body was wrapped in burlap, and the gravesite was filled with charcoal. Once his body was lowered into the grave, liberal amounts of brandy were poured over it. The gravesite was properly marked, and the wagon train proceeded along the trail. During the winter, Susano returned with a group of men and exhumed the body, which was found in an almost perfect state of preservation. The body of Manuel Salustiano Delgado travelled back to Santa Fe and was buried in the San Miguel Cemetery with a proper funeral service.

With population growth, the custom of underground church cemeteries began to change by the 1800s, although exceptions were made for clergy, who continued to be buried beneath the church. Like roots spreading from a tree, these

Manuel Salustiano Delgado was a prominent trader who died in the 1830s along the Santa Fe Trail. His body was later buried in the San Miguel Cemetery in Santa Fe. *Courtesy of J. Paul Taylor's family archives.*

Cemeteries that were built in the proximity of a Catholic church were called *camposantos*. This is a 1912 photograph by Ina Sizer Cassidy of the cemetery behind the San Miguel Chapel in Santa Fe. *Courtesy of the Palace of the Governors [NMHM/DCA]. No. 030011.*

new cemeteries extended from the church property and were known as the *camposanto* (consecrated ground). The location of the *camposanto* served a dual purpose: it provided protection against attacks from marauding Natives as the colonists sought protection within the confines of the church during the funeral, and more importantly, people believed that burial within close proximity to the church would help with their salvation in the next world. The area immediately surrounding the place of worship became a part of the spiritual center of the community, where memories of the dead continued to be nurtured on consecrated ground. A new tradition also began during this time that was in keeping with a colonial beliefs: during the construction of the church, the workers would carve the initials of the deceased into the mud of the adobe bricks used for the church walls to ensure that the prayers of the living would benefit the souls of the dead.

As the population continued to grow, burial grounds began to be built farther away from churches, and the tradition of the funeral procession began to flourish. The European practice of funeral processions began in Santa Fe in 1598, when Don Juan de Oñate and the founding families settled the region for the Spanish Crown. It was an inherited tradition that began with St. James, the patron saint of Spain. When St. Peter became the first pope, it was the duty of St. James to spread the teachings of Christianity; he was martyred for his efforts by King Herod. Each year on October 12, Spain honors his legacy with an elaborate procession. During the first two hundred years of New Mexico's history, it was under Spanish and Mexican rule and Catholicism was the only religion practiced. At this time in Catholicism, all types of processions, especially those performed at funerals, were an integral part of daily life. On the solemn walk from the church to the *camposanto*, the deceased were carried on an *escalera* (ladder) and wrapped with a *serape* (blanket). During the procession, the *dolientes* (mourners) would stop to rest and say a *sudario* (prayer) for the deceased, and they would mark the spot with a flagstone that had a cross etched into it, thus creating a *descanso* or a place of rest.

From the sixteenth century until the mid-nineteenth century, the Spanish people of New Mexico were isolated from the rest of the world and the guiding hand of the church. Through the growth of colonization, some small communities began to establish themselves even farther away from the larger villages that had a community church. Groups of men in these villages formed a religious brotherhood known as Los Hermanos Penitentes, whose roots can be traced to the medieval *cofradias* of Spain. The concept of death figured prominently in their religious practices. Along with images of the crucifixion of Christ, their *moradas* (meetinghouses) also contained skulls and other imagery associated with death. The brotherhood of the

The Spanish tradition of religious processions was an integral part of daily life in New Mexico. This 1895 funeral procession took place in Mora, New Mexico. *Courtesy Palace of the Governors [NMHM/DCA]. No. 014757.*

This image shows the Penitente brotherhood presiding over a graveside funeral service circa 1890 in northern New Mexico. *E. W. Cosner Collection, Courtesy of the Special Collections of the Center for Southwest Research [UNM Libraries]. No. 2009-002-0003.*

Penitentes would conduct spiritual services at the *moradas*, which were often surrounded by a *camposanto*. Burials often took place in the immediate vicinity of the *morada*, which was considered holy ground, just as it was in villages with larger populations and a church. The Penitentes served the needs for these communities in times of bereavement. In New Mexico, the Penitentes continue to play an important role in their communities, with their *moradas* coming to life during Holy Week. Throughout the year, the organizations contribute to their communities' well-being by helping the disadvantaged, sick and elderly.

Since Catholicism was the only religion of New Mexico for two hundred years, the first Catholic cemetery to serve the burial needs of Santa Fe surrounded the San Miguel Mission. Early documents indicate that the church was built by the Franciscan missionaries between 1605 and 1608. The mission church was located on the south side of the Santa Fe River in the Barrio de Analco, which is an Aztec phrase that means "the other side." It became the primary place of worship for missionaries, their Native converts and the community of Santa Fe throughout the seventeenth century. Reputed to be the oldest church in the United States, the San Miguel Mission

The cemeteries of the Penitentes were usually built in the immediate vicinity of the *morada*, which was considered holy ground. This image shows a Ranchos de Taos *morada* and cemetery as they appeared in 1972. *Courtesy of the Palace of the Governors [NMHM/ DCA]. No. 147090.*

In New Mexico, the Penitentes continue to play an important role in their communities. In this photograph, a group of people gather at the *morada* in northern New Mexico during Holy Week services. *Courtesy* La Herencia *Photo Archives.*

This photograph is of a funeral procession in 1917 at Isleta Pueblo. The deceased is shown being carried on an *escalera* (ladder). *Courtesy Palace of the Governors [NMHM/ DCA]. No. 036309.*

was burned during the 1680 Pueblo Revolt, but it was not completely destroyed. The thick adobe walls had not been affected by the fire, and the destruction was limited to the wooden roof and framework. When de Vargas restored Spanish control in New Mexico in 1692, he ordered that the church be repaired. In 1859, the church was used as a chapel for the newly arrived Christian Brothers. In its long history, the church has served as a mission, a barrio church, a military chapel, an oratory for the Christian Brothers and a revered shrine to St. Michael, the patron saint of the dying.

On November 22, 1859, four French La Sallian Christian Brothers arrived in Santa Fe with the task of founding El Colegio de San Miguel adjacent to the San Miguel Mission. The new school for boys included boarders from around the state. By 1867, the reputation of the institution had grown to the point that the infrastructure of the school could not keep pace with the increased enrollment, and its infrastructure began to deteriorate. The school's water supply became contaminated with a mysterious diarrheal disease that afflicted many of the students and resulted in the deaths of two of them. To avoid further contagion, the boys were buried in haste in the cemetery surrounding the church. When Doña Maria Gertrudis Peña de Sanchez, the mother of one of the dead students, arrived in Santa Fe from the family's ranch in northern New Mexico, she was horrified to learn that the graves had not been identified and that she would never know the exact location of her son's final resting place. Doña Maria never returned to her family's ranch and instead devoted the rest of her life to the memory of her son. Day after day, she went to the cemetery to pray the rosary over the two gravesites; she hoped her prayers would intercede on behalf of the soul of her son. The New Mexico State PERA (Public Employees Retirement Association) building was constructed on the land of the old Santa Fe cemetery near the San Miguel Mission. Throughout the years, rumors have circulated that the PERA building is haunted. On more than one occasion, people have claimed they saw a Spanish woman, who was dressed in attire from a different era and wearing a *mantilla* (a lace head covering), disappear through the building's walls. Many believe this apparition to be the ghost of the distraught Doña Maria, who continues to roam the building in search of the grave of her son.

Through the mid-twentieth century, Hispanics in Santa Fe continued to practice the funeral traditions of medieval Spain, which included believing in the superstitions associated with death. In the 1940s and 1950s, the community believed that they had their own Angel of Death, a mysterious man by the name of Alejandrito. It is said that he roamed the streets of town with an uncanny knack of knowing when someone was about to die. People feared his presence and would say, *"Alla anda Alejandrito rodeando las animas. ¿Quién se ird a morir?"* Which translates to, "Alejandrito is gathering the souls of the departed. I wonder who will die next?" Alejandrito was born on Alto Street near Our Lady of Guadalupe Church. He was referred to as an *innocente*, a person of limited mental capacity, and he was mute. He was born into a poor family and always wore hand-me-down clothes and a large dark overcoat, which he placed over layers of other coats, regardless of the season. He stood five feet and seven inches high, was very thin and had a sunburned, weathered face from years of living on the street. Not much else was known about him except that when someone died, no matter what part of Santa Fe they were in, Alejandrito was at their house within hours. He would stay with the mourners and lead the funeral procession to the cemetery. The community of Santa Fe believed that God spoke to Alejandrito and told him when someone was going to die. On one cold winter morning in 1960, Alejandrito was found frozen to death at the Santa Fe River by Our Lady of Guadalupe Church, not far from the home where he was born. For the man who attended so many funerals and consoled the bereaved, no one was there when he died.

In 1868, Our Lady of Guadalupe and Rosario Cemeteries were established as Catholic cemeteries for the city of Santa Fe. At the turn of the twentieth century, the Spanish families living in the northeastern corridor of Santa Fe established the Cristo Rey Cemetery on land that was a part of the Rodriguez Land Grant for stillborn infants and loved ones of the victims of the 1918 worldwide influenza epidemic. The small cemetery contained about one hundred graves when Cristo Rey Church was built in 1939. The surnames of the families buried there include Apodaca, Armijo, Gonzales, Padilla and Rodriguez. Following the end of World War II in 1945, the Archdiocese of Santa Fe made the decision to consolidate its Catholic burial grounds and closed both Our Lady of Guadalupe and Cristo Rey cemeteries. All Catholic burials were directed to Rosario Cemetery, which is still in use today and is the city's oldest continuous cemetery.

Rosario Cemetery is located on the grounds where Diego de Vargas encamped with his army when they arrived in September 1692 to resettle Santa Fe after the Pueblo Revolt of 1680. Rosario Chapel is located in the northwest corner of the cemetery. The original church was built under the direction of de Vargas in gratitude for the resettlement of the capital city. It was built as a shrine to La Conquistadora, the oldest Madonna in the United States, who accompanied de Vargas. By the early part of the nineteenth century, the chapel had fallen into disrepair and had to be rebuilt in 1807. Spanish families sought out the best burial plots in close proximity to the chapel so that they could be near La Conquistadora. A special section at the cemetery next to Rosario Chapel is reserved for the Sisters of Loretto and the La Sallian Christian Brothers. Both of these religious orders came to Santa Fe in the 1850s at the behest of Archbishop Jean Baptiste in order to create a new educational system. The Sisters of Loretto were the first to arrive in 1852. After establishing a school in Santa Fe, the Sisters also founded academies in Albuquerque, El Paso and Denver; they did all of this during an era in which most girls didn't have the opportunity to get an education. The La Sallian Christian Brothers opened St. Michael's College for boys and young men in Santa Fe in 1859. Their mission was to continue the work of its founder, St. John-Baptist de Salle, who opened his first school in 1679 in Reims, France. The Christian Brothers also founded a four-year college in 1947, in Santa Fe, which was formally called St. Michael's College before being changed to the College of Santa Fe. The college closed its doors in 2009. Today, St. Michael's High School is one of the hundreds of schools in

Right: The cemetery for Cristo Rey Church began at the turn of the twentieth century but closed following the end of World War II. *Photograph by Ana Pacheco.*

Below: There are only a few tombstones visible at the Cristo Rey Cemetery on Camino Ribera; the rest have been covered by the proliferation of trees in the cemetery. *Photograph by Ana Pacheco.*

Our Lady of Guadalupe was one of the main cemeteries in Santa Fe until it closed in the 1940s. *Photograph by Ana Pacheco.*

As the city of Santa Fe continued to grow, the property of Our Lady of Guadalupe's cemetery has been engulfed by commercial real estate. *Photograph by Ana Pacheco.*

eighty different countries that continue to provide the educational vision of its French founder. In 1969, St. Michael's High School became a coeducational institution after Loretto Academy closed.

There are many historical gravesites at Rosario Cemetery, including a memorial to men lost in battle during World War II. At least two men who were interred at the Japanese internment camp during World War II are buried in a field at the cemetery next to the Santa Fe National Cemetery. In 1942, an executive order signed by President Franklin D. Roosevelt was issued through the Department of Justice to purchase the Civilian Conservation Corps (CCC) camp north of Santa Fe to be used to incarcerate Japanese Americans who had ancestors from what was considered a foreign enemy during World War II. These Japanese Americans were forcibly removed from different parts of the country, mostly the West Coast; they were forced to leave their families, businesses and all ties to the community. The newly transformed CCC facility became the Japanese internment camp, one of several opened throughout the country in areas considered to be of military importance for the safety of all Americans. Within weeks, 4,555 men were imprisoned at the camp. These so-called enemy combatants were teachers, journalists, businessmen

This 1934 photograph shows the Santa Fe Christian Brothers. *Courtesy of the New Orleans–Santa Fe Christian Brothers District Archives.*

Above: A memorial tombstone for the Sisters of Loretto at Rosario Cemetery. *Photograph by Ana Pacheco.*

Left: A memorial cross at Rosario Cemetery for the Christian Brothers of Santa Fe. *Photograph by Ana Pacheco.*

A monument at Rosario Cemetery honoring the World War II soldiers who never returned or were presumed dead. *Photograph by Ana Pacheco.*

and artists, people who the American government felt posed a threat because they were free thinkers.

Other notable people buried at Rosario Cemetery are the photographer Robert H. Martin, who was instrumental in documenting the dawn of the atomic age. In 1946, the young soldier was sent to Los Alamos National Laboratory to record the Manhattan Project. The following year, the army ceded control of the project to the U.S. Atomic Energy

These tombstones at Rosario Cemetery belong to two Japanese prisoners who died while incarcerated at the Japanese internment camp during World War II. *Photograph by Ana Pacheco.*

Commission, but Martin chose to stay in his role as a private citizen, a job that he maintained for thirty years. Martin worked with a contingent of scientists from around the world who were chosen to work on both nuclear and hydrogen bombs. In 1949, he documented their work at Eniwetok Atoll in the Pacific Ocean. In addition to his work for the lab, he did photographic projects for the USO during World War II. Robert H. Martin provided a historical account of Santa Fe and northern New Mexico for six generations until his death in 2005.

Concha Oritz y Pino de Kleven, the most influential Hispanic woman in New Mexico during the twentieth century, is also buried at Rosario Cemetery. She was born in 1910 to a wealthy family that had deep political roots in New Mexico. Her great-great-grandfather Don Pedro Bautista Pino represented New Mexico in 1810, when the Spanish Court convened in the city of Cortes. It was a historical event, since Pino was the first native-born New Mexican to give an account of life in the Spanish outpost. From that moment on, a member of the Pino family has played an important role in New Mexican politics. When Concha was a young woman, she ran Agua Verde, the family's one-hundred-thousand-acre ranch that spread across three counties, and she also ventured into the world of politics. In 1941, Concha became the first female majority whip of the New Mexico state

Buddhist teachers were among the men incarcerated at the Japanese internment camp in Santa Fe. From 1942 to 1946, 4,555 Japanese men were imprisoned at the camp in the northern part of the capital city. *Photograph courtesy of manymountains.org.*

The photographer Robert H. Martin caught in an air-bound pose at the White Sands Monument in the 1940s. *Photo by Mela Martin. Courtesy* La Herencia *Photo Archives.*

The tombstone of Robert H. Martin at Rosario Cemetery. *Photograph by Ana Pacheco.*

legislature and the first woman to hold that position in the United States. A champion of women's rights, Concha served under the direction of five presidential administrations: Kennedy, Johnson, Nixon, Ford and Carter, who all appointed her to national boards that fought for the handicapped, the humanities and the arts. When she died in 2006, she was an active member of sixty national and local boards that work for the betterment of society.

As a more diverse population began to settle in Santa Fe following its inclusion as a U.S. territory, the first non-Catholic cemetery was established by the Masons and Odd Fellows in 1853. In 1884, the Fairview Cemetery was also added to the list of cemeteries in Santa Fe and was built on the northwestern part of town to accommodate the growing population; it is still in use today. Fairview was the first cemetery to reserve a Jewish section for burial. Memorial Gardens Cemetery, located in the southeastern part of Santa Fe, was established in the 1950s; it also had a Jewish section. The settlement of New Mexico's Ashkenazi Jews from Germany and other European countries began with the merchants who trekked the Santa Fe Trail from 1848 to 1871. Many chose Santa Fe as their new home when

Concha Ortiz y Pino de Kleven and a worker tend to the spring lambs at the Agua Verde Ranch. *Courtesy of the Palace of the Governors [NMHM/DCA]. No. 059021.*

The tombstone of Concha Ortiz y Pino de Kleven at Rosario Cemetery in Santa Fe. *Photograph by Ana Pacheco.*

they reached the end of the trail. Santa Fe's growth stagnated in 1878, when the railroad bypassed the city in lieu of Las Vegas sixty miles to the north. Las Vegas became a major commercial hub with a large Jewish community that operated mercantile businesses. In 1881, the Montefiore Cemetery was created, and it was one of the first Jewish cemeteries west of the Mississippi.

Since their arrival, the Jewish spirit of community collaboration has spurred their involvement in all civic affairs. One of their most significant contributions to the city occurred during the construction of the Cathedral Basilica of St. Francis of Assisi. In need of financial assistance to complete the construction, Archbishop Jean Baptiste Lamy sought financial help from Jewish merchants. In gratitude for their assistance, the area above the doors of the main entrance is inscribed with the ancient Hebrew Tetragrammaton "YHWH," meaning "God's existence."

In 2013, the funeral of Santa Fe's first full-time rabbi was held at the Basilica Cathedral of St. Francis of Assisi. It was the first time in the history of Santa Fe that a Jewish funeral was held at a Catholic church. Rabbi Leonard A. Hellman had attended major religious holidays at the cathedral.

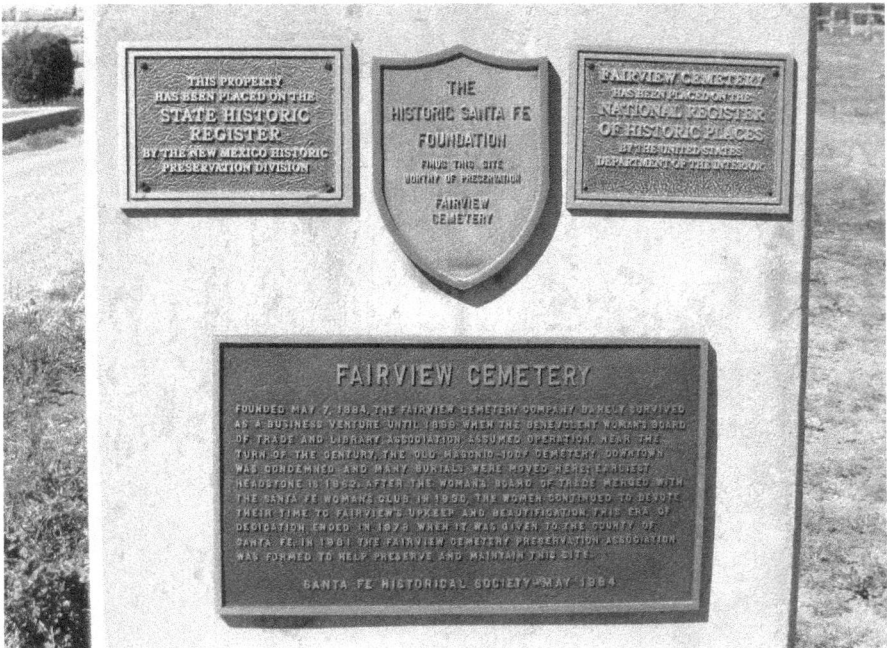

The Fairview Cemetery, founded in 1884, was the first permanent non-Catholic cemetery in Santa Fe, and it is still in use today. *Photograph by Ana Pacheco.*

This image shows a memorial sponsored by the Jewish Community Council of Northern New Mexico in the Jewish section of Memorial Gardens Cemetery in Santa Fe. *Photo by Ana Pacheco.*

The Star of David is featured in the center of a contemplation circle in the Jewish section of Memorial Gardens Cemetery. *Photo by Ana Pacheco.*

He appreciated the Christian iconography, music and ceremonial rituals. His final request was that his funeral be held at the cathedral. In a fitting farewell, his coffin was carried through the doors on which the word "God" was written in the language of his faith.

Like Rosario Cemetery, Fairview also has gravesites of historical note. The Staab family, who were some of the earliest traders to arrive on the Santa Fe Trail, have a family plot. Carlos Vierra, the first commercial artist to arrive in Santa Fe, is buried there, as are author Margaret Laughlin and photographer Christian G. Kaadt. Charles W. Dudrow came to Santa Fe between 1869 and 1872; he had been a driver for the Barlow and Sanderson stage lines that ran from Pueblo, Colorado, to Santa Fe. When he arrived in Santa Fe, he married Cora Bear and became a business partner with her father, Samuel Bear. They opened the Dudrow & Bear Transfer Corral in 1881, located near the train depot and Our Lady of Guadalupe Church.

Jesus Sito Candelario was one of the most successful curio merchants in New Mexico. He opened his shop in the late 1880s on San Francisco Street, where the façade of his curio shop is still located today. Candelario

Rabbi Leonard A. Hellman was Santa Fe's first full-time rabbi. When he died in 2013, he requested that his funeral be held at the Basilica Cathedral of St. Francis of Assisi. *Photo courtesy of the* La Herencia *Archives.*

The tombstone for Rabbi A. Hellman at Memorial Gardens with the epitaph "Fear Not Death." *Photo by Ana Pacheco.*

Zadoc Staab and his brother, Abraham, were major suppliers of dry goods for the military during the Civil War. They went on to become the largest wholesale traders in the Southwest. *From left to right:* Bernard Seligman, Zadoc Staab and Lehman Spiegelberg with Kiowa Indian scouts. *Courtesy of the Palace of the Governors [NMHM/DCA]. No. 007890.*

Left: The tombstone of Abraham Staab in the family plot at Fairview Cemetery. *Photograph by Ana Pacheco.*

Below: The Dudrow & Bear Transfer Corral, in 1881, was located near the train depot and Guadalupe Church. Charles W. Dudrow and his father-in-law opened the business in 1881. *Photograph by Ben Wittick. Courtesy of the Palace of the Governors [NMHM/DCA]. No. 015826.*

The Dudrow family tombstones at Fairview Cemetery. The tombstone on the right (shaped like a tree stump) is that of Charles Dudrow, who co-founded Dudrow & Bear Transfer Corral in 1881. *Photograph by Ana Pacheco.*

prospered where many had failed, because he had empathy for the Native Americans and worked directly with members of the surrounding Pueblo tribes. His grandson John S. Candelario was born in Santa Fe on September 7, 1916, and from an early age, John helped his grandfather in the shop. Jesus Sito taught him the importance of understanding and respecting the Native way of life. The education John received in his formative years went on to serve him greatly when he became a professional photographer. By 1954, John's photographs had been exhibited at the Museum of Modern Art in New York. The images he captured of northern New Mexico were published in several major magazines around the country. Candelario also became a cinematographer, receiving both an Emmy and a Peabody Award for his work. His reverence for Native American cultures was illustrated in a 1943 interview with *Minicam Photography* magazine when he said:

> *The Southwest seems disconnected from the rest of the country because it is so different, so untouched by civilization and the noise of cities. A mile*

beyond the city limits, you would never dream there could be a city there; it rises before you like a vision from some fairy tale. Only the Indians belong to this country, and it has left its mark upon them too deeply to ever be erased. Something of the quietness of the landscape is reflected in their faces. The photographer can catch their expressions, but the artist with the camera can disclose their character.

Throughout his successful career, Candelario remained a local boy and died in Santa Fe in 1993.

Santa Fe's National Cemetery began as the battlefields of the American Civil War continued to move westward. The Confederate soldiers who were killed during the Battle of Glorieta Pass in 1862 were reburied on grounds next to Rosario Catholic Cemetery with a memorial dedicated

Left: The tombstone of Jesus Sito Candelario at Fairview Cemetery. *Photograph by Ana Pacheco.*

Below: The tombstone of John S. Candelario is next to that of his grandfather Jesus Sito Candelario at Fairview Cemetery. *Photograph by Ana Pacheco.*

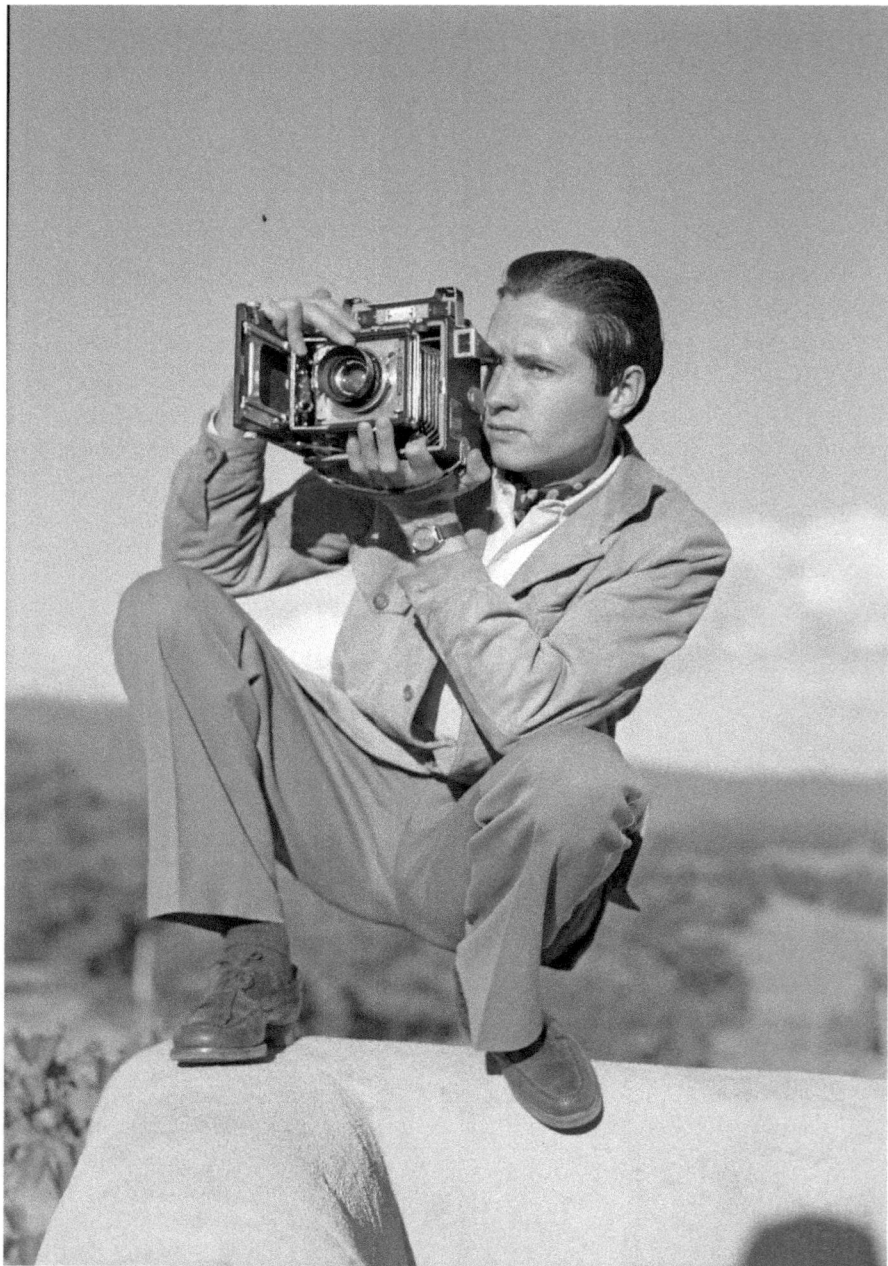

John S. Candelario was an award-winning photographer who achieved national recognition in the 1940s. *Courtesy of the Palace of the Governors [NMHM/DCA], No. 177045.*

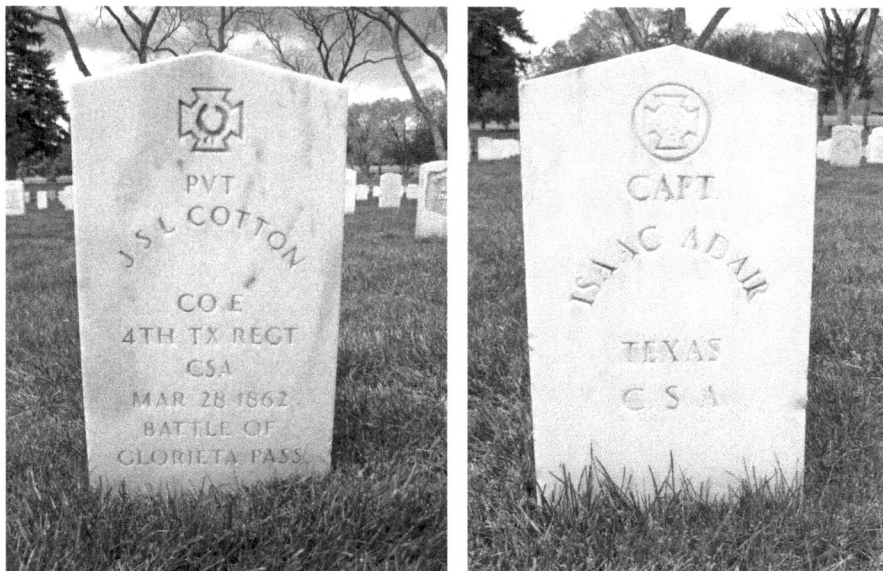

These are the tombstones of two Confederate soldiers who were killed at the Battle of Glorietta Pass on March 28, 1862, at the Santa Fe National Cemetery. *Photograph by Ana Pacheco.*

to the conflict. Eight years later, the Archdiocese of Santa Fe donated that land to the federal government for use as a national cemetery. By 1885, the government brought the remains of soldiers who had been buried at old military outposts to the Santa Fe National Cemetery for reinterment. The earliest graves of the cemetery can be traced back to both the Civil War and Native campaigns. The Santa Fe National Cemetery has the largest burial ground for veterans in the state. The property consists of 78.6 acres, and it is where more than 65,000 veterans of all branches of the military are buried. Approximately 1,800 interments are conducted annually.

Some of the earliest burials at the cemetery were those of members of the Tenth Cavalry Regiment, known as the Buffalo Soldiers. The military contingent was given this sobriquet by the Native Americans because their hair reminded the Natives of buffalo fur. Several African American regiments were formed during the Civil War shortly after Congress established the first peacetime all-black regiments in the U.S. Army. This particular division of the U.S. Army was one of the few African American contingents that served during the Indian and Spanish-American Wars. They provided protection to western settlers from marauding Indians and Mexican bandits during the era of Manifest Destiny and westward expansion. The remains of sixty-

This is a 1945 photograph of a World War II soldier and his friend in Galisteo, New Mexico. *Photograph by Robert H. Martin. Courtesy of* La Herencia *Photo Archives.*

These are the Buffalo Soldiers of Troop L, one of several African American military units formed by Congress after the Civil War. *Courtesy of the Palace of the Governors [NMHM/DCA]. No. 098373.*

four Buffalo Soldiers who died at the Fort Craig military outpost southeast of Santa Fe were reinterred at the National Cemetery. These soldiers are buried below the Fort Craig monument.

Ten Medal of Honor Recipients, whose service records date back to the Indian Campaigns of 1868, are also buried at the Santa Fe National Cemetery. The Medal of Honor is the military's preeminent award to service members who distinguish themselves through acts of remarkable heroism. Several memorials honoring the men and women of the United States Armed Forces can be found at the cemetery, as well as the countless tombstones of unknown soldiers. The Navajo Code Talkers Monument honors the courage and sacrifice of the approximately three hundred Navajo Code Talkers who served in the Pacific Theater of World War II. These Navajo soldiers transitioned from life on the reservation to the arduous realities of wartime in the Marine Corps. The U.S. Armed Forces faced tremendous challenges in the Pacific because Japanese intelligence consistently infiltrated American military strategies, which resulted in the loss of many American lives. The Navajo soldiers became indispensable assets as they transmitted crucial wartime information in their native language of Diné, which the enemy

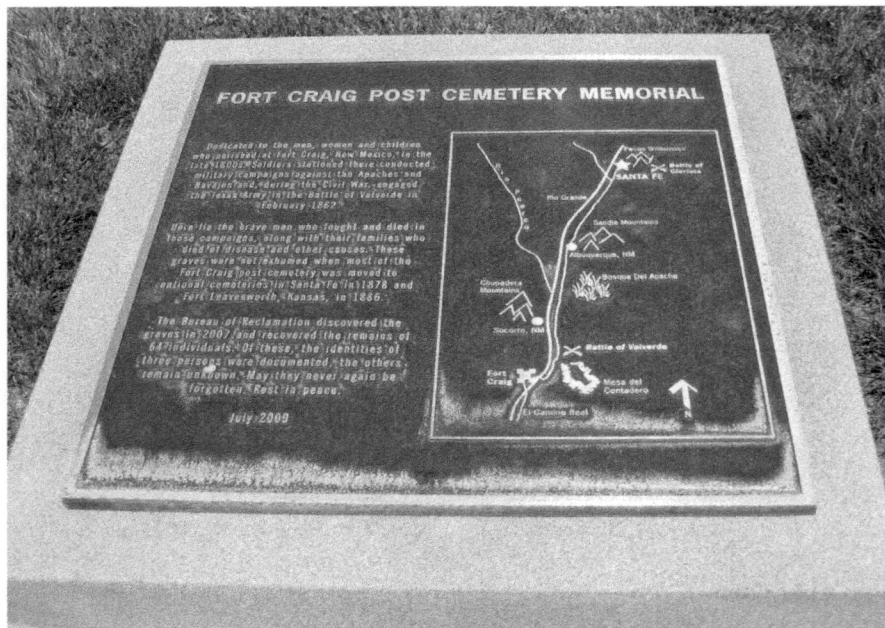

This is a photograph of the Fort Craig Post Cemetery Memorial at the Santa Fe National Cemetery, where sixty-four Buffalo Soldiers are buried. This monument is dedicated to the men, women and children who perished at Fort Craig in the late 1800s. *Photograph by Ana Pacheco.*

forces were unable to decipher. Diné not only lacked a written language, but it was also totally foreign to the enemy code crackers. The Navajo Code Talkers became America's secret weapon to gaining a foothold toward victory. Fifteen of the Code Talkers are buried at the Santa Fe National Cemetery, including Chester Nez, who was one of the last survivors of the original twenty-nine Code Talkers.

Three other World War II monuments are featured at the Santa Fe National Cemetery: the World War II Glider Pilots monument honors the 5,500 glider pilots who transported troops and equipment to battlefields in Europe, including the invasions of Sicily and Normandy; the men and women who served in the China-Burma-India theater during World War II are also honored with a memorial at the cemetery; and there is a memorial to the navy branch of Women Appointed for Voluntary Emergency Service (WAVES). Women serving in the military dates back to the Revolutionary War, when they functioned primarily as nurses, a tradition that continued through World War I. It wasn't until the Second World War that women in

Left: One of several tombstones at the Santa Fe National Cemetery for the unknown soldiers killed in battle. *Photograph by Ana Pacheco.*

Below: The Navajo Code Talkers played a crucial role in military intelligence during World War II. This image shows a memorial honoring these Navajo soldiers at the Santa Fe National Cemetery. *Photograph by Ana Pacheco.*

the navy were given other duties. Women served in the Korean War but were forbidden from enlisting in the Vietnam War. Today, women proudly serve in every branch of the military.

It is mandated that all national cemeteries use the same, uniform headstones that are furnished by the government, but in the early days of the Santa Fe National Cemetery, some wealthy families decided to use their own headstones. The most unique of these private markers is that of Private Dennis O'Leary. The young soldier was stationed at Fort Wingate, 190 miles west of Santa Fe, where he died in 1901, supposedly of tuberculosis. However, history has a way of embellishing facts. Legend has it that when

Top: The memorial tombstone at the Santa Fe National Cemetery for the glider pilots killed during World War II. *Photograph by Ana Pacheco.*

Middle: The Santa Fe National Cemetery tombstone honoring the men and women who served in the China-Burma-India theater during World War II. *Photograph by Ana Pacheco.*

Bottom: The memorial tombstone at the Santa Fe National Cemetery commemorating the women who served in the military. *Photograph by Ana Pacheco.*

The tombstone of Private Dennis O'Leary, who served at Fort Wingate, is one of the few statues permitted at the Santa Fe National Cemetery. *Photograph by Ana Pacheco.*

Private O'Leary was bored, he would venture into the mountains, where he began to carve a statue of himself. It is said that when he completed the monument, he shot himself on April 1, 1901 (April Fools' Day). He is supposed to have left a suicide note with the location of his statue and a request that it be placed on his grave.

The early residents of Albuquerque were buried in front of San Felipe de Neri Church on the west side of the Old Town Plaza. The church was built in 1706, when New Mexico's largest city was founded, but by 1793, the church had deteriorated, and a new church was built on the north side of the plaza. A new cemetery was created for the church that grew from the south and west to the edge of the old church cemetery. As the two cemeteries merged to capacity, an additional burial ground was created two blocks north, across from Mountain Road. From its creation, the new cemetery never held the reverence of the church cemetery. Many of the graves there were unmarked, and the surrounding area was unfenced, allowing animals to graze and trample on burial sites. As Albuquerque became the economic hub of the state, its population continued to grow, so the Santa Barbara Cemetery was established three miles east of San Felipe de Neri. Church officials exhumed the graves of the surrounding church cemetery and took the remains in a procession to the Santa Barbara Cemetery, where they were reburied. The people buried near Mountain Road received a less dignified reinterment. The San Felipe de Neri congregation was outraged to learn that the church leaders had sold the cemetery to a farmer without notifying the parishioners. The farmer had agreed in a written statement that he would transport any bones found while working the land for burial at the Santa Barbara Cemetery. He dug up the bones of hundreds of people, loaded them into his wagon and dumped them into a mass grave at Santa Barbara without a proper or honorable burial. The community suffered this tragedy without any recourse but to pray for the souls of generations of family members.

Remnants of the *conversos*, the hidden Jews of New Mexico, can be found carved on the headstones at *camposantos* throughout the northern part of the state. Many are engraved with both the Star of David and the Catholic cross, evidence of the dual faith that they practiced. Just as the Native Americans were forced to convert to Christianity while honoring their own spirituality secretly, many of New Mexico's first Spaniards also practiced a hidden faith. They were Sephardic Jews who had fled the Inquisition under the guise of being *conversos*, Jews who had converted to Catholicism.

The Star of David was carved into the cross over Isabel Romero's grave in a cemetery in Truchas, New Mexico. *Courtesy of* La Herencia *Photo Archives.*

Left: Catholics in New Mexico believe that when a child dies, they immediately go to heaven. The image of an angel is often found at the gravesite of a child to indicate that they have become angels. *Courtesy of* La Herencia *Photo Archives.*

Below: Stuffed toys adorn the gravesite of a child at this *camposanto* in northern New Mexico. *Courtesy of* La Herencia *Photo Archives.*

Above: A metal replica of a motorcycle adorns a gravesite in northern New Mexico. Car and motorcycle parts left at gravesites may indicate the deceased's love for a certain vehicle or that they died as a result of a vehicular accident. *Courtesy of* La Herencia *Photo Archives.*

Left: *Farolitos* (little lanterns) adorn this gravesite. They are lit on Christmas Eve. *Courtesy of* La Herencia *Photo Archives.*

They became known as Crypto Jews, because they practiced their Jewish faith covertly while presenting a different persona in public. It wasn't until the mid-twentieth century that revelations of their existence came to light. Virtually all of the descendants of the Crypto Jews were buried through the Catholic Church, but remnants of their religious roots can be found on their gravesites.

Another unique aspect of the *camposanto* is the attention and nurturing that is given to each gravesite, especially those of children. These burial grounds are often filled with elaborately carved crosses and other grave monuments; fresh flowers adorn the graves in the summer and are replaced with plastic flowers during the colder months. It is considered a sacrilege to disrespect a *camposanto*, and the disinterment of a grave cannot proceed for any reason without the permission of a family member. Today in New Mexico, the word *camposanto* not only applies to the consecrated burial grounds surrounding churches but also to any cemetery by those who still speak Spanish. Families share in the responsibility of maintaining the *camposanto*, many of which are located on private properties for the burial of family members only. With the personal care given to the final resting places of loved ones, gravesites begin to take on lives of their own. Elaborate detail is given to each grave, with sentimental memorabilia like teddy bears, photos, car wheels and motorcycle rims. Often, these solemn grounds bring cheer, with epitaphs like "Gone Fishing" or, as in the case of a gravesite that contained a battery-operated sign, "Santa, Stop Here."

There is an ongoing New Mexican tradition to gather and spend time with deceased loved ones and decorate their gravesites on Christmas Eve. Preparations for the celebration begins in the late afternoon by lining the graves with *farolitos* (little lanterns), small paper sacks filled with sand and candles. The *farolitos* are then lit during the evening to welcome the birth of the Christ child and honor the memory of their dead family members. The traditional flowers associated with death in New Mexico, Mexico and other cultures throughout the world are *cempasuchil* (marigold flowers), but on Christmas Eve, they are replaced with poinsettias and miniature Christmas trees. Christmas ornaments and candy canes also adorn graves. During the Christmas Eve celebration at the *camposanto*, families sing and play recorded versions of religious songs, Christmas tunes and the Spanish song *Las Mañanitas*, the traditional birthday song.

5
BENEATH THE SURFACE

Geographically, New Mexico is the fifth-largest state in the country after Alaska, Texas, California and Montana. Buried in the swathe of more than 121,000 miles of sand and caliche are countless lives that have traipsed its boundaries from the four corners of New Mexico, Utah, Arizona and Colorado to the border of Mexico.

These lives include those of the area's first inhabitants, the ancient Pueblo people, who succumbed to death while in search of food and shelter. The Spanish colonists followed in 1598, with many dying on La Jornada del Muerto (the Journey of the Dead), the 1,500-mile-long Camino Real. A fractious melding of these two groups resulted in the deaths of the twenty-one Franciscan friars who lost their lives during the 1680 Pueblo Revolt. They are memorialized in the state's capital of Santa Fe with the Cross of the Martyrs monument, which overlooks the city. Ironically, no memorial exists in northern New Mexico for the thousands of Native Americans who died during that conflict, nor are there any memorials devoted to the many other brutal Native deaths that occurred at the hands of their occupiers. As time passed, more battles ensued, which prematurely zapped the lives of many. The Battle of Glorieta Pass, which occurred on March 28, 1862, is known as the "Gettysburg of the West." The battle took place 25 miles southeast of Santa Fe during the American Civil War; the Confederate army bore the brunt of casualties with the loss of more than one hundred men. Through war, famine, drought, epidemics and life's inevitable aging process, millions of lives have ended in New Mexico. Buried beneath the

The Cross of the Martyrs in Santa Fe is a memorial to the twenty-one Franciscan friars who perished during the Pueblo Revolt of 1680. *Courtesy of the Palace of the Governors [NMHM/DCA]. No. 052455.*

state's magnificent vistas are the people who became a part of history in small and big ways that endure today.

The Cross of the Martyrs, located north of the Santa Fe Plaza, is a memorial to the twenty-one Franciscan priests who lost their lives during the Pueblo Revolt. From 1680 to 1692, the Pueblo tribe successfully drove the Spanish colonists out of New Mexico to El Paso del Norte (or El Paso, Texas, which was then a part of Mexico). The Pueblo Revolt was undoubtedly the most significant event to shape the history of New Mexico. When the Spaniards arrived in 1598, they enslaved the Natives, forced them to convert to Catholicism and burned their sacred objects and underground ceremonial chambers (*kivas*). By 1676, the harsh treatment of the Natives by the colonists reached a climax when forty-seven Pueblo religious leaders were falsely accused of witchcraft and flogged publicly in Santa Fe. One of the men persecuted was Po'pay, who led the revolt four years later. At that time, there were eighteen Pueblo tribes throughout the state, and all of them participated in the uprising. The first blood of the revolt was shed at Tesuque Pueblo on August 9, 1680, with the killing of a Spaniard named

Cristobal de Herrera. Twelve years later, in 1692, the rule of the Spanish Crown was restored in New Mexico when Diego de Vargas regained control of the Spanish settlement of Santa Fe.

Conflict with nomadic Natives persisted in Santa Fe and its surrounding areas through the next century. In 1806, the Louisiana Purchase brought the first American explorers to New Mexico when Lieutenant Zebulon Pike and his men crossed the San Luis Valley into the northern part of the state. By 1821, the Santa Fe Trail, which began in Franklin, Missouri, and ended in the Santa Fe Plaza, issued in a new era of people coming from the east. In 1848, New Mexico became a U.S. territory. Pope Pius IX appointed Jean Baptiste Lamy as bishop to Santa Fe in 1850; when Lamy arrived the following year, he quickly went to work establishing the first archdiocese in the area and building the Romanesque cathedral that is now known as the Basilica Cathedral of St. Francis of Assisi. The new church was erected in the exact location of La Parroquia, Santa Fe's parish church that was established during the seventeenth century. The subterranean burial chambers of the first church remained, and new burial chambers were added during the construction of the cathedral. Archbishop Jean Baptiste Lamy became the first bishop to be buried underneath the cathedral in 1888.

Gertrudes Barcelo was an unprecedented exception to the rule that only the clergy were to be buried beneath the cathedral. During the heyday of travel along the Santa Fe Trail, in the 1840s and 1850s, Barcelo operated a gambling hall and brothel in Santa Fe. Doña Tules, as she was known, was an expert at the card game Monte and was purported to be the power behind the throne as the mistress of Governor Manuel Armijo, the last New Mexico governor under the rule of the Mexican government. She was a shrewd businesswoman whose success grew with the occupation of the U.S. government. In 1847, she warned American authorities of an impending plot to overthrow the new government, which she knew would impact her gambling empire. Quickly becoming the wealthiest woman in Santa Fe, Doña Tules had made a fortune of more than $10,000 and owned several houses. Suddenly, she also became accepted in circles of high society and was given the honorific of Señora Doña Gertrudes Barcelo. The clergy remained tolerant of her livelihood and accepted her good deeds in society and the generous contributions she gave to the Catholic Church. When she died in 1852, her funeral was one of the most elaborate spectacles of the time, costing more than $400, which would be the equivalent of $13,000 in today's economy. High-ranking members of the church, military officers

Right: Archbishop Jean Baptiste Lamy lying in state at Loretto Chapel on February 14, 1888. Lamy was the first bishop to be buried underneath the Basilica Cathedral of Francis of Assisi. *Photograph by Brother Amian. Courtesy of the Palace of the Governors [NMHM/DCA]. No. 55185.*

Below: The coffin of a Franciscan friar in a burial chamber below the Basilica Cathedral of St. Francis of Assisi. *Photograph by Jesse Nusbaum. Courtesy of the Palace of the Governors [NMHM/DCA]. No. 061446.*

and throngs of spectators from Santa Fe and the surrounding villages attended her funeral. Along with being buried in regalia that was normally associated with royalty, her final wish was to be buried underneath La Parroquia. It is there, among the hierarchy of the church, that Doña Tules found eternal peace.

Padre Antonio Jose Martinez has gone down in the annals of New Mexico history as a priest, a father to several children, a man of letters, an astute politician and, some say, a traitor. In 1830 and 1836, Martinez was the deputy of the Assembly of the Department of New Mexico under the Mexican government. The controversial priest established a printing press in 1835, which was the first in New Mexico and the first west of the Mississippi River. He published *El Crepúsculode la Libertad*, a newspaper that he used as a venue for his political views and to take aim at his critics. In the following decade, he advocated for the annexation of the Territory of New Mexico by the United States. Although he was one of the most prominent Mexican citizens in favor of the new government, he was falsely accused of being one of the instigators of the Revolt of 1847 against the American government and the assassination of Governor Charles Bent. Padre Martinez was never convicted and died shortly thereafter in Taos, New Mexico.

At the age of fifteen, Christopher "Kit" Carson had his eyes set on Santa Fe and ran away to join a wagon train bound for the capital city. Along the Santa Fe Trail, he quickly became a trapper, soldier and Indian agent. Later, he married an Arapaho woman, and his second wife was Cheyenne. Ironically, while he was working to better the lives of Natives, he also was also waging a brutal campaign against the Navajo, destroying their crops and villages. In 1864, Carson was in charge of removing the Navajos from their native land; he forced them to walk three hundred miles to Bosque Redondo south of Santa Fe in what is now known as the Long Walk. Carson was also a war hero, and in 1884, a monumental obelisk at the federal courthouse in Santa Fe was erected in honor of his bravery in the Mexican-American and Civil Wars. Kit Carson died in 1868, and he was buried in Taos at the Kit Carson Park and Cemetery. A museum bearing his name is also located in Taos.

In 1864, Lucien B. Maxwell was the largest land grant owner in the world. His was a rags-to-riches story, and it started when he was born in Illinois in 1818 to a family of Native American traders. At the age of seventeen, Maxwell embarked on an adventure west as a trapper and met the dynamic frontiersman Kit Carson. Enthralled with the escapades of Carson, Maxwell followed him to Taos, New Mexico. While he was there, Maxwell was

Left: Padre Antonio Jose Martinez was a priest, politician and publisher who established the first printing press in New Mexico in 1835. *Courtesy of the Palace of the Governors [NMHM/DCA]. No. 11262.*

Right: The grave of Padre Antonio Jose Martinez in Taos, New Mexico. Martinez died in 1847 under a cloud of suspicion. He was one of the instigators of the Revolt of 1847 against the American government. *Courtesy of the Special Collections of the Center for Southwest Research [UNM Libraries]. No. 994-014-Taos-0009.*

introduced to the enterprising businessman Carlos Beaubien and quickly went to work for him. Maxwell fell in love with Beaubien's thirteen-year-old daughter, and with her father's blessing, the forty-two-year-old Maxwell was married to Maria de la Luz by Padre Jose Antonio Martinez in 1862. Beaubien was an astute businessman who petitioned for a land grant that was composed of property in northern New Mexico and southern Colorado during the Mexican-American War. Maxwell inherited the land grant and took over the family business, supplying food and supplies to the troops during the American Civil War, after his father-in-law died. In 1868, gold was discovered on the Maxwell land grant, and the property was leased to miners and their families. Maxwell provided housing, food and supplies to the miners. During the first year of operation, Maxwell's mine, which was called the Aztec Mine, had produced $1 million worth of gold, making Maxwell a very wealthy man. With his newfound prosperity, Maxwell

Christopher "Kit" Carson is seated in the middle of this 1866 photograph of military personnel at the Masonic Temple in Santa Fe. All of the officers featured in this photograph were veterans of both the Mexican-American War and American Civil War. *Seated, left to right:* Colonel D.H. Rucker, Kit Carson and Brevet Brigadier General James Carleton. *Standing, left to right:* Colonel E.H. Bergmann, Delegate Charles P. Clever, Colonel Nelson H. Davis, Colonel Herbert M. Enos, Surgeon Basil K. Norris and Colonel J.C. McFerran. *Photograph by Nicholas Brown. Courtesy of the Palace of the Governors [NMHM/DCA]. No. 009826.*

invested in a number of different business ventures. He founded the First National Bank of Santa Fe in 1867, but he soon found that he did not have the business acumen to make the bank successful and sold it. After selling the bank, Maxwell became a cattle rancher and invested in other agricultural ventures, but they all failed. By 1870, he had lost all of his assets, and he died five years later in poverty. Maxwell's child bride, Maria de la Luz, was buried by his side at the Old Fort Sumner Cemetery twenty-five years later. In 1879, the town of Maxwell in Colfax County was named in his honor.

On March 1, 1873, Reverend David F. McFarland performed a marriage ceremony for Kathrine McCarty and William Antrim in the sanctuary of the First Presbyterian Church in Santa Fe. It was a second marriage for Kathrine, who had been widowed nine years earlier. Her two sons, Henry

This circa 1890 photograph shows the gravesite of Kit Carson, who died in 1868. The gravesite is located in Taos at the Kit Carson Park and Historic Cemetery. *Courtesy of the Palace of the Governors [NMHM/DCA]. No. 047604.*

The gravesite of Lucien B. Maxwell at Fort Sumner, New Mexico. In 1864, Maxwell was the largest land grant owner in the world. *Courtesy of the Special Collections of the Center for Southwest Research.*

and Joe, stood as witnesses to the ceremony. After her first husband died in New York City, she took the boys west, where she met William Antrim. Kathrine suffered from advanced tuberculosis and hoped her new husband would love and care for the boys if anything happened to her. After the wedding, they moved to the drier climate of Silver City, where she hoped that her sons would lead Christian lives. Kathrine died the following year, when her eldest son turned fourteen. Henry was close to his mother and was devastated by her death. The boys' stepfather abused the two teenagers, and without a moral compass, Henry began a life of petty crime. His first offense was stealing clothes from a Chinese laundry; after he was arrested, he escaped from the jailhouse through its chimney. That was the beginning of his life as a criminal in New Mexico and Arizona, where he soon became known as Billy the Kid. In the seven years that followed, Billy the Kid created a larger-than-life persona that continues today. After killing eight men by the age of twenty-one, Billy the Kid was captured and sentenced to death by hanging. At his sentencing, the judge reportedly said, "You will hang until you're dead, dead, dead." Billy the Kid retorted back at the judge, "And you can go to hell, hell, hell."

Two weeks before his scheduled execution, the escape artist managed to get away again, killing two guards in the process. Sheriff Pat Garret tracked

Born William Henry McCarty in 1859, Billy the Kid died in 1881. *Courtesy of the Palace of the Governors [NMHM/DCA]. No. 03079.*

him down to the Maxwell Ranch in Fort Sumner, New Mexico, where he shot and killed Billy the Kid on July 14, 1881. The life of one of the West's most notorious outlaws may have ended abruptly, but Billy the Kid's infamy lives on. William Henry McCarty was buried at the Old Fort Sumner Cemetery, not far from the grave of Lucien Maxwell. His mother, Kathrine, rests eternally 395 miles to the west at the Memory Lane Cemetery in Silver City.

D.H. Lawrence, the English author and poet, and his wife, Frieda, lived intermittently in Taos, New Mexico, from 1922 to 1925. The couple was invited to New Mexico by wealthy socialite Mable Dodge Luhan, who hosted several intellectuals and artists during that era. The couple's time in New Mexico was a much-needed respite from the tensions they endured while living in Europe during World War I. At that time, Lawrence's book *Lady Chatterley's Lover* was considered pornographic and had created a lot of controversy. In addition to this scandal, Lawrence had always been vocal in his opposition to the war, and his wife was German, so the couple was falsely accused of being spies. Their 160-acre Flying Heart Ranch in Taos was the only property the couple ever owned. They obtained the ranch from Luhan in 1924 in a barter arrangement, in which she was given Lawrence's manuscript of his 1913 autobiographical novel *Sons and Lovers*. The book was published to great critical acclaim and was made into a movie in 1960. The couple renamed the land Kiowa Ranch after the Kiowa Indians who had inhabited the land from AD 1050 to 1225. The property was located near the 120-mile Kiowa Trail that intersected with the Camino Real, the Santa Fe Trail and the Old Spanish Trail. Lawrence died from tuberculosis on March 2, 1930, in Vence, France. Five years later, Frieda had his body exhumed, cremated and brought to his home in New Mexico, which is now called the D.H. Lawrence Ranch, 18 miles northwest of Taos.

In the late 1890s, Edgar L. Hewett discovered black shards of pottery at Chaco Canyon that dated back to the Southwest's Neolithic Period. The anthropologist sought the assistance of Maria Martinez of the San

The memorial tombstone for Billy the Kid and his friends Tom O'Folliard and Charlie Bowdre at the Old Fort Sumner Cemetery. *Courtesy of the Palace of the Governors [NMHM/ DCA]. No. 177709.*

The original tombstone for Kathrine Antrim, Billy the Kid's mother, at Memory Lane Cemetery in Silver City, New Mexico. *Courtesy of the Palace of the Governors [NMHM/ DCA]. No. 093140.*

Above: An updated granite tombstone for Kathrine Antrim's gravesite. *Courtesy of the Palace of the Governors [NMHM/DCA]. No. 093140.*

Left: English author D.H. Lawrence and his wife, Frieda, lived in Taos, New Mexico, from 1922 to 1925. D.H. died in 1930 in France, and his ashes are interred at the D.H. Lawrence Ranch, eighteen miles northwest of Taos. *Photograph by Witter Bynner. Courtesy of the Palace of the Governors [NMHM/DCA]. No. 200135.*

Ildefonso Pueblo to revive this ancient technique of black-on-black pottery from the Stone Age. By the time Martinez had died in 1980, this type of Pueblo pottery had become world-renowned. Hewett was also instrumental in convincing the U.S. Congress to pass the American Antiquities Act of 1906, which made it illegal to pillage ancient ruins. In 1907, Hewett founded the School of American Archaeology, which is now called the School of Advanced Research, and in 1909, he also founded the Museum of New Mexico. When Hewett died in 1946, his ashes were interred at the museum, surrounded by the art that continues to define Santa Fe as one of the most prominent art markets in the country.

On August 9, 1944, the U.S. Forest Service created an ad campaign using a fictional bear as part of a promotion to prevent forest fires. Six years later, in the spring of 1950, word of a bear cub that had barely survived a forest fire in New Mexico reached the Washington, D.C. offices. The singed baby bear was found by firefighters clinging to life in a charred tree. The rescue team fell in love with the five-pound cub and named him Smokey Bear while nursing him back to health. Smokey was flown to the nation's capital

The anthropologist Edgar L. Hewett founded the Museum of New Mexico in 1909. When Hewett died in 1946, his ashes were interred at the Museum of New Mexico. *Photograph by Jesse Nusbaum. Courtesy of the Palace of the Governors [NMHM/DCA]. No. 007383.*

and took up residence at the National Zoo. Smokey Bear became the living symbol of the danger and devastation of forest fires, and for the next twenty-five years, he was an American icon. The ad campaign "Only You Can Prevent Forest Fires," featuring Smokey Bear, earned more than $1 million in promotion for the Forest Service. When Smokey died of natural causes on November 9, 1976, his obituary was prominently featured in the *Washington Post*, and his death was mourned nationally. The Forest Service flew his body back to New Mexico for interment in the Capitan Mountains, where he had been found twenty-six years earlier. In 1979, the Smokey Bear Historical Park opened in Capitan, New Mexico, where his legacy continues to grow with the park. Smokey Bear Historical Park has become the most widely visited tourist attraction in south-central New Mexico.

Georgia O'Keeffe's love affair with New Mexico began in 1929 on her first visit to the state. By 1940, O'Keeffe had purchased property in Abiquiu at Ghost Ranch, a sprawling twenty-one-thousand-acre ranch run by the Presbyterian Church. After the death of her husband, Alfred Stieglitz, in 1946, O'Keeffe moved permanently to her ranch in Abiquiu, where she spent the rest of her life. It was Stieglitz who propelled her career as one of the most important female artists of the twentieth century; her paintings of skulls and flowers have become a synonymous representation of the American Southwest. The Georgia O'Keeffe Museum, which opened in Santa Fe in 1997, is the most widely attended cultural institution in the state, and in 1998, her Abiquiu home was designated a National Historic Landmark. In accordance with her wishes, when she died in 1986, her body was cremated, and her ashes were scattered at the top of Pedernal Mountain near her home in the expansive northern New Mexico vista that she immortalized in her paintings. That area is now often referred to as "O'Keeffe Country."

New Mexico's best-known author, Tony Hillerman, was born on May 27, 1925, in Sacred Heart, Oklahoma. From the age of five to thirteen, Hillerman was one of a few boys who attended St. Mary's Academy, a boarding school for Native American girls. It was during those formative years his bond was solidified with the Native people of the Southwest. Hillerman was a recipient of the Silver Star, Bronze Star, Oak Leaf Cluster and Purple Heart for his service during World War II. After returning from the war, Hillerman received a degree in journalism in 1948 and worked for newspapers in Oklahoma, Texas and New Mexico. He was a reporter for the *Santa Fe New Mexican*, where he worked his way up to become the editor. In 1963, he moved his family to Albuquerque to pursue a degree in creative writing with the dream of becoming a novelist. For the next two decades,

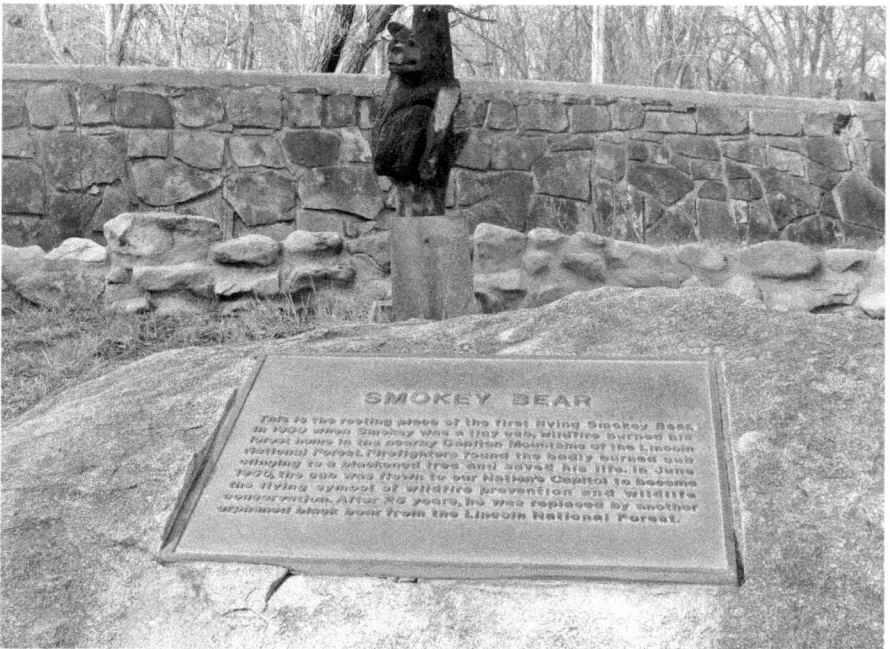

SMOKEY BEAR

This is the resting place of the first living Smokey Bear. In 1950 when Smokey was a tiny cub, wildfire burned his first home in the nearby Capitan Mountains of the Lincoln National Forest. Firefighters found the badly burned cub clinging to a blackened tree and saved his life. In June 1950, the cub was flown to our Nation's Capitol to become the living symbol of wildfire prevention and wildlife conservation. After 26 years, he was replaced by another orphaned black bear from the Lincoln National Forest.

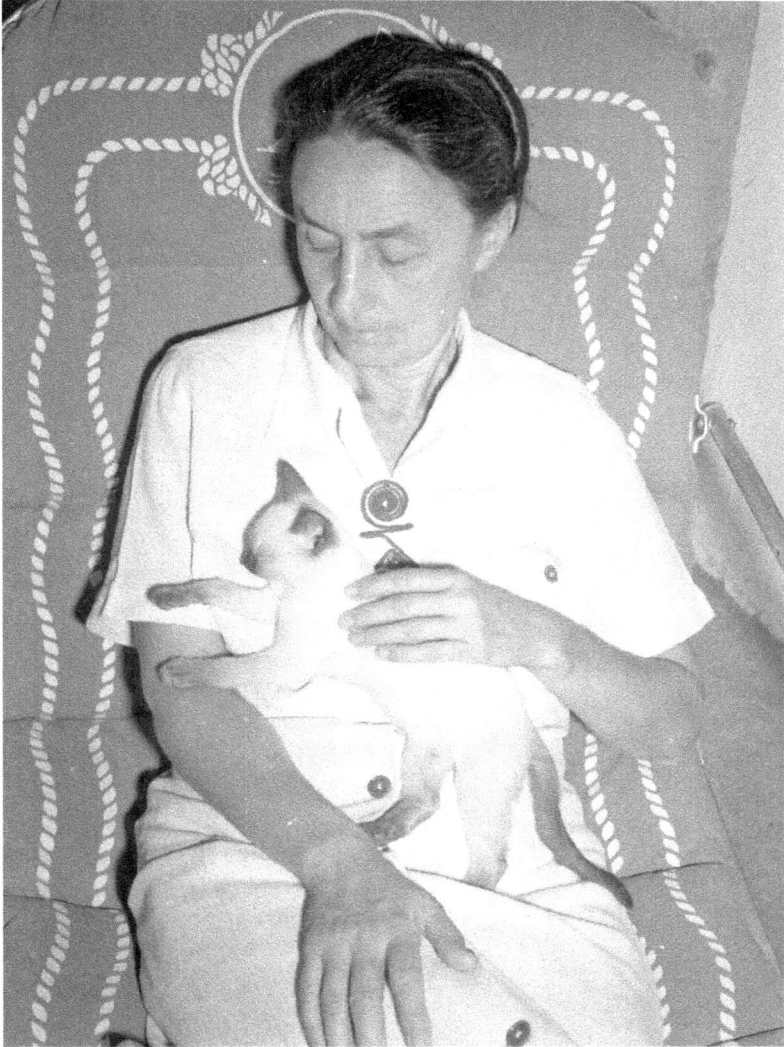

Above: Georgia O'Keeffe died in 1986, and her ashes are scattered at the top of Pedernal Mountain near her home in the expansive northern New Mexico vista. This area was immortalized in her paintings and is often referred to as "O'Keeffe Country." *Photograph by John Candelario. Courtesy of the Palace of the Governors [NMHM/DCA]. No. 165660.*

Opposite, top: A 1950 U.S. Forest Service promotional photo featuring Smokey Bear. *Courtesy of the Palace of the Governors [NMHM/DCA]. No. PA-MU-154.*

Opposite, bottom: The Smokey Bear Historical Park opened in Capitan, New Mexico, in 1979. It is there that the legendary icon for the U.S. Forest Service is entombed. *Courtesy of the Smokey Bear Historical Park.*

Tony Hillerman was an award-winning author who deftly spun the ethnographic landscape of the Southwest into an award-winning mystery series. *Courtesy of the Hillerman family.*

Hillerman was also a professor of journalism at the University of New Mexico. His most popular fictional work was about the Navajo reservation of northeastern Arizona and northwestern New Mexico. From 1970 to 2006, Hillerman produced thirty-seven original works, which included eighteen works of fiction, two children's books, screenplays and five nonfiction pieces. All of his works depicted the people and terrain of New Mexico, introducing them to the world. He died on October 26, 2008, and was buried at the Santa Fe National Cemetery.

The Bosque Redondo Memorial was created in 2005 by the New Mexico State Monuments Division and the Museum of New Mexico in acknowledgement of the brutal treatment sustained by the Navajo and Mescalero Apache tribes from 1863 to 1868 at the hands of the U.S. government. Located 165 miles southeast of Santa Fe in De Baca County, Fort Sumner was established by Congress on October 31, 1862, as the first Native reservation west of Oklahoma Territory. During America's westward expansion in the 1860s, the Native people of the region fought to keep their land and traditional way of life. The U.S. Army retaliated by destroying their villages, crops and livestock. The surviving Navajo people were starved into submission and relocated to Fort Sumner. In 1864,

A 1945 World War II photograph in Europe of Tony Hillerman at a pinning ceremony for his heroic service. *Courtesy of the Hillerman family.*

more than 8,500 Navajo men, women and children were forced to walk 300 miles to the fort during the winter. Many of the prisoners died of exposure and starvation along the way. The brutal treatment of the Native people on this arduous journey, which has come to be known as the Long Walk, is one of the darkest stains on U.S. history.

The Navajo people endured dismal conditions at Fort Sumner, and many of them succumbed to malnutrition and disease. Both the Mescalero Apache and Navajo tribes were relocated to Fort Sumner under the guise of a promised peace treaty with the American government that would soon return them to their native lands. However, the United States reneged on that promise because rich mineral resources, including gold and silver, were discovered in those native territories. It was not until 1868 that the government finally conceded that its plan to relocate the tribes to a single reservation was ill conceived and unsustainable given the poor agricultural conditions of the location. When the Apache and Navajo people were allowed to return to their homelands, they soon discovered that the size of their territory had been greatly reduced through the encroachment of the American Homestead Act of 1862, which encouraged settlers to migrate west. The tribes were diminished in size but not in spirit; they slowly rebuilt their lives, leaving a part of their legacy at Fort Sumner, where hundreds of their people died under the oppression of the U.S. government.

A plaque honoring the New Mexico Volunteers who fought at the Battle of Glorieta Pass is located at the Pecos National Historical Park thirty miles southeast of Santa Fe. During the 2019 New Mexico legislative session, a new bill was proposed to create a memorial at the site of the Battle of Glorieta Pass. The new memorial would honor the Hispanic soldiers who played a key role in helping the Union army gain control of the West. Initially, the Confederate army had established a stronghold in New Mexico, and its flag was flown in the Santa Fe Plaza for three weeks. But after the Battle of Glorieta Pass, the Union soldiers were empowered to take Sante Fe back with the aid of Hispanic soldiers who volunteered to help their cause.

During World War II, on April 9, 1942, the entire platoon of the 200th Coast Artillery, which consisted of 1,800 New Mexicans, was captured by the Japanese army. They became part of a contingent of 75,000 prisoners of war who were forced to walk sixty miles to Camp O'Donnell in central Luzon in the Philippines. Without sufficient food and water, many of the soldiers fell behind from exhaustion and were bayoneted to death during the walk. In 1989, the annual White Sands Bataan Death March Marathon was created to honor the New Mexican veterans of the Bataan Death March. In the spring, people from around the world join together in the desert at White Sands to remember the anniversary of one of the greatest tragedies of World War II. Both civilians and military personnel carry heavy backpacks through the desert with the option of doing either a 15.4- or 26.2-mile hike that both begin at 6:30 a.m. The New Mexico National Guard sets up relief tents to aid the walkers who return from their journey dehydrated and with blisters on their feet. The participants' maladies are but an inkling of what the soldiers endured during the arduous sixty-mile march of 1942.

To commemorate the sixtieth anniversary of the Bataan Death March, in 2002, the first federally funded memorial was created at Veterans Park in Las Cruces, the state's second-largest city. As a part of that commemoration, a portion of U.S. Highway 70 from Las Cruces to Alamogordo was named Bataan Memorial Highway. In Santa Fe, the building that served as the New Mexico State Capitol from 1900 to 1966 was renamed the Bataan Memorial Building. The Bataan Death March is considered one of the most brutal chapters of American military history, and New Mexico bore the brunt of these casualties with nine hundred men from New Mexico's 200th Coast Artillery perishing.

NEVER TO BE FORGOTTEN

The wooden carvings of Doña Sebastiana were the symbolic images of death used in Hispanic New Mexico through the mid-nineteenth century. This allegorical icon of death used by the Penitente brotherhood was the feminization of St. Sebastian, an Italian saint martyred with arrows for his efforts to spread Christianity in AD 283. The image of Doña Sebastiana, or La Muerte as she is also known, is presented in three ways: as a skeleton wearing a black shroud and carrying an arrow to represent the swiftness of death and its ability to strike anyone at any time; as a skeleton that is blindfolded to suggest that people are blind to the realization that death can occur at any moment; and as a skeleton in a cart holding a bow and arrow to symbolize that life (the cart) is moving inevitably toward death. The symbolism of La Muerte and her death cart dates back to the Spanish Inquisition and the Black Plague that decimated Europe from 1347 to 1350. During the epidemic, the dead were transported to mass burials in carts. Historically, the *carreta* (cart) is also symbolic of early death practices in New Mexico. The two-wheeled wooden cart was brought to the Americas by the Spanish colonists during their expedition of 1598. As they traveled the 1,500-mile Camino Real, the carts were often used to carry the people who died along the route. Rather than risk an attack by Natives in daylight, the dead were placed in the *carreta* to be pulled along by the oxen until their burial at night.

While colonial New Mexico was reminded of death through the artistic carvings of Doña Sebastiana, their wealthy counterparts in Spain and

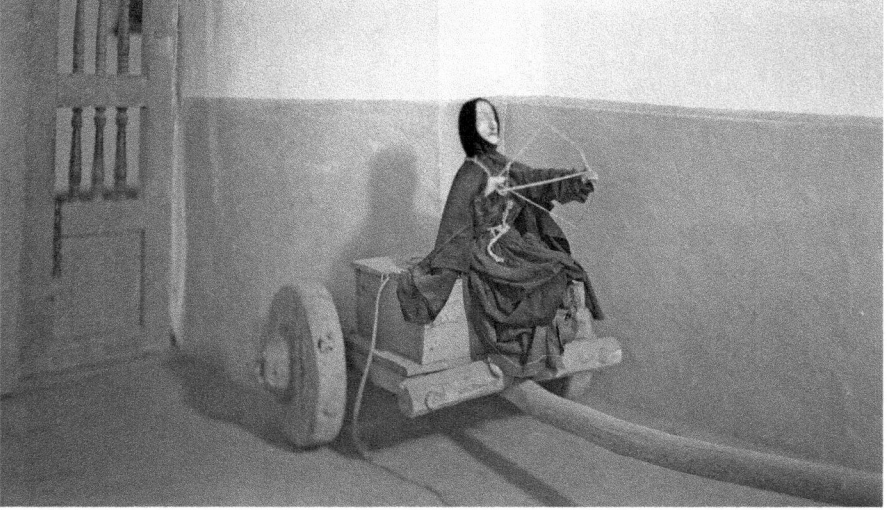

A 1935 photograph in Trampas, New Mexico, of Doña Sebastiana, the allegorical icon of death for the Penitente brotherhood. *Photograph by T. Harmon Parkhurst. Courtesy of the Palace of the Governors [NMHM/DCA]. No. 011529.*

The symbolism of La Muerte and her death cart dates back to the Spanish Inquisition and the Black Plague that decimated Europe between the years 1347 and 1350. *Courtesy of the Palace of the Governors [NMHM/DCA]. No. 86116.*

Mexico commissioned artists to create postmortem portraits of their deceased loved ones. These artists worked in the presence of corpses, and they often peeled back the eyelids to get the correct eye color, since the paintings of the deceased almost always depicted them with their eyes open, as if they were still alive. In addition to paintings, clay masks and sculptures were also made to memorialize the dead; they wanted to make sure that the face of a loved one would never be forgotten.

It wasn't until the invention of the daguerreotype in Europe in the early 1830s and the advent of photography in 1839 that the concept of having a final image of a loved one began to take root. By 1851, photographs of the Santa Fe Plaza and surrounding areas were being captured by curious and adventurous photographers who made their way to the capital city in covered wagons on the Santa Fe Trail. In the beginning, very few people could afford to have photographs taken, so only the wealthy had their images captured on film. Soon, however, the thought of forgetting the face of a loved one who had died justified the expense of such an extravagance.

By the end of the nineteenth century, taking photographs with the dead had become a part of the funeral tradition. *Courtesy of* La Herencia *Photo Archives.*

By the end of the nineteenth century, this new technology became accessible to most socioeconomic segments of the population, and photographing the dead became intertwined with the grieving process in New Mexico.

The most common photographs of the dead were those of infants and children. As there was a high infant mortality rate, the photographs allowed parents to have an image of their child who would never grow up. The loss of a child was a devastating experience, and people consoled themselves in the belief that children under the age of eight, who had received the sacrament of baptism, went straight to heaven and became angels. The bodies of these *angelitos* were kept at home in the living room, where they remained for a couple of nights. This way, friends and relatives were able to visit and pray with the family to ask the Infant of Prague to carry the soul of the child directly to heaven, where the angels would greet them. The photographs of these children in their coffins, dressed in satin with floral crowns arranged on their heads, were often the only images that their grieving families would ever possess of them. Siblings and other family members were often photographed with the dead children.

Photographs of deceased family members were prominently displayed next to photos of the living. These photos held a place of honor in the home and served as a vital part of the grieving process. By remembering the dead through conversation and sharing pleasant accounts of their lives at family gatherings, people believed they could keep the departed spiritually alive. Photographs of the dead surrounded by family members were often taken because it was the families' last chance to have a complete family photo. For young children who had lost a parent or grandparent, these photographs were their last memories of that relative. Photographing the dead allowed the memory of the departed to live on with future generations. Paintings of the deceased tried to disguise death, while photographs preserved it. Like embalming, photographing the dead momentarily stopped the ravages of decay by capturing one final image. In addition to having these photos on display, families also kept them in albums along with images of the living. As time passed and people in the "living photographs" also died, a black cross would be marked over their chest to indicate that they were no longer among the living. Family photos with the dead were also taken at cemeteries to capture the final moments before the departed disappeared into the earth. As the availability of photography became more widespread, other cultures in New Mexico began to document gravesite memorials.

Through the mid-twentieth century, the traditions carried out when burying dead children included an array of flowers in their coffins and a floral crowns on their heads. *Courtesy of* La Herencia *Photo Archives.*

Japanese immigrants and other migrant groups found work in the mines and on the railroads during the latter part of the nineteenth century. Gold and silver were discovered in 1880 in the San Mateo, Magdalena and Black Range Mountains south of Albuquerque, which created an economic boom for the region. When the Atchison, Topeka and Santa Fe Railroad made its way to New Mexico the following year, a polyglot of cultures arrived from both Asia and Europe. They came to work as carpenters, quarrymen, miners, fieldworkers, cooks, barbers, seamstresses, shopkeepers, laundries, bartenders and even prostitutes.

Family members pose for a photograph with their father at his funeral in 1931. *Courtesy of* La Herencia *Photo Archives.*

Children pose with their grandfather at his funeral in 1931. Photographing the dead allowed memories of the departed to be passed down to future generations. *Courtesy of* La Herencia *Photo Archives.*

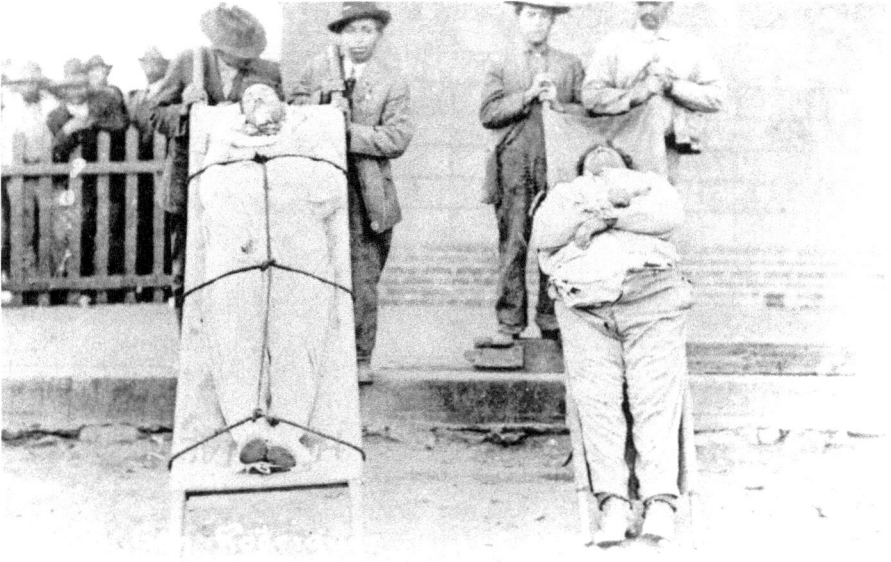

A photograph of the bodies of General Rodriguez and Colonel Baca-Valles in March 1917. They were casualties of the Mexican Revolution. *Courtesy of* La Herencia *Photo Archives.*

A Japanese graveside funeral in southern New Mexico. Photographing the service at the cemetery allowed the camera to capture that final moment before the deceased disappeared into the earth. *Photograph by Robert L. Campbell. Courtesy of the Palace of the Governors [NMHM/DCA]. No. HP.2015.26.041.*

In the early years of photography, the camera required long exposure times to capture each image. The dead made this extended wait time easier for the photographer, since they didn't fidget. Photographs of the dead with their eyes closed were also better for the families, since it gave the subject the appearance of being asleep. On occasion, families requested that their dead children appear alive, so eyes would be painted on the photograph once it was developed. As the popularity of this type of photography grew, studios began making cards of these images to be given to friends and relatives. Like the iconography of Doña Sebastiana, these *memento mori* cards were meant for the living. *Memento mori* is derived from the Latin phrase that means "Remember, you must die."

DISEASE AND DEMISE

According to a recent study by researchers at Harvard University, the Native population in North America was estimated to be between 2 and 18 million people prior to the 1492 arrival of Christopher Columbus. By the end of the nineteenth century, that population had dwindled to about 530,000 people. In New Mexico, in a period of just sixty years (from 1620 to 1680), the combined population of the eighteen Pueblo tribes had gone from around 6,500 to fewer than 900 people. The demise of the Native population was a byproduct of this nation's first settlement in New Mexico, one of the earliest points of European contact in the United States. Along with bringing livestock and tools that were new to the region, the Spanish colonists introduced old-world diseases to the unsuspecting Native population. Prior to colonization, the Native people did not suffer from smallpox, measles, chickenpox, influenza, typhus, diphtheria, cholera, bubonic plague, scarlet fever, whooping cough or malaria. Virtually 95 percent of the Native American population was decimated within the first 150 years of European occupation. In a period of just two years (from 1780 to 1782), a smallpox epidemic wiped out 50 percent of the Pueblo population in northern New Mexico. In the following century, outbreaks of cholera gravely afflicted the region due to a lack of sufficient sanitation systems. In the early part of the twentieth century, the worldwide influenza epidemic of 1918, which killed approximately 50 million people, found its way to New Mexico. The wrath of this epidemic did not discriminate; from New Mexico's largest city of Albuquerque to the state's small villages in the north, New Mexicans were impacted. Quinine was used as a remedy to ward off the virus, households suffering from the sickness were quarantined and the doors and windowsills of the sick were layered with creosote to limit the spread of germs. During the epidemic, schools, public buildings and churches were closed. There were no funerals for the dead. Men with cloths wrapped around their faces came to collect the remains, placing them in sacks. With the large number of deaths, there was a shortage of coffins and no time to make new ones. There were so many deaths in such a short period of time that communities had to resort to mass burials. When winter came, the illness seemed to have finally run its course, and people welcomed the cold weather, believing that it was the snow that killed the virus.

Unlike some early diseases that killed off large segments of the community in a short period of time, tuberculosis actually added to New Mexico's population. After Mexico gained its independence from Spain in 1821, trade opened between New Mexico and the United States. William Becknell, known as the father of the Santa Fe Trail, arrived in Santa Fe with a smattering of wagons that contained hardware, lumber, cotton, wool

The people of New Mexico believed that it was the snow that finally stopped the influenza epidemic of 1918. *Courtesy of the Palace of the Governors [NMHM/DCA]. No. 061447.*

and other much-needed products. For the next half century, the Santa Fe Trail became the lifeline of New Mexico, and the caravans of wagons grew larger, hauling manufactured goods from the east. Along with the surplus of supplies, a small group of mostly young, pale-faced men began to arrive. These men were suffering from tuberculosis. Because of their white pallor, the disease was called the "White Plague," and the arrival of these men brought the dreaded lung disease to the region. Only a few of those afflicted men actually survived long enough to reach New Mexico, but when the railroad arrived in 1880, hundreds of people suffering with tuberculosis began to arrive.

Tuberculosis destroyed the lungs and was referred to as "consumption," since those stricken with it experienced extreme weight loss. The disease became synonymous with death, because little was known about treating the mysterious disease. From the late nineteenth century until 1940, tuberculosis was the leading cause of death in the United States. It was observed during that era that people with tuberculosis seemed to fare better in the high-altitude terrain of the West. The densely populated cities in the East were rife with contagion, while New Mexico's sparsely populated communities provided pristine air, low humidity and endless days of sunshine.

With the arrival of the "lungers," grave suspicion arose. Many establishments, from boardinghouses to restaurants, prohibited people suffering with tuberculosis. Even hospitals had to institute guidelines when treating tuberculosis patients in order to protect everyone else in the hospital. People believed that they could contract the disease from sufferers' incessant coughing and excretion of phlegm, which proved to be a correct assumption. By 1907, New Mexico had joined several other states in the region that had already passed laws prohibiting public spitting. In spite of the collective fear that tuberculosis had created, an entire industry was created from this disease, and the people in New Mexico learned to adjust to these new arrivals for economic reasons.

Many of these sufferers were young men from upper-middle-class, educated families, who came with enough money to weather through their illness. The railroad was a booming business that herded consumptives to the state. When sufferers arrived, they required housing, food and other necessities, so businesses like hospitals, hotels and boardinghouses prospered. Funeral homes also flourished, since many of the sick died within thirty days to six months after their arrival. Cities like Albuquerque, Santa Fe, Silver City, Ruidoso and Taos advertised their curative facilities in publications in the East, which attracted even more people. By the 1920s, approximately 10 percent of New Mexico's population was composed of people suffering from tuberculosis.

The advent of penicillin finally put an end to the scourge of tuberculosis, but until the antibiotic became widely available in the 1940s, New Mexico's tuberculosis sanatoriums gained a reputation for curing the disease. The state's claim that its pristine air, low humidity and abundant sunshine were beneficial to the patients during their lengthy convalescences turned out to be true. Once they recovered, a large percentage of the younger patients decided to make New Mexico their permanent home. Like the economic benefits they provided when they were sick, their contributions to the state once they recovered proved to be exceedingly beneficial. From medicine to civics and the arts, many of the state's leading citizens had once suffered from tuberculosis.

Clinton P. Anderson came to Albuquerque from South Dakota in 1917. At the time, he was twenty-two years old with advanced tuberculosis. His prognosis was grave, and he was told that his days ahead were limited. But the young man never gave up hope, and he continued to live one day at a time. Through months of rest and recovery, Anderson grew stronger, and when he recovered, he made Albuquerque his new home and started an insurance company. During the Great Depression, Anderson entered the political arena and became the state treasurer, where he administered federal relief programs. Following that position, he was elected to Congress, and by 1949, Anderson was elected to the U.S. Senate, an office he held until his retirement in 1973.

Bronson Cutting arrived in New Mexico in 1910 with a degree from Harvard University. Born into a wealthy New York family, Cutting had the pedigree and connections for a bright future, but fate dealt him a different hand when he contracted tuberculosis. Fortunately, Cutting did recover and became the publisher of the *New Mexican* and *El Nuevo Mexicano*, the Spanish-language version of the newspaper, in Santa Fe in 1912, the same year that New Mexico became a state. His journalism career was put on hold when World War I broke out and he joined the army. Cutting attained the rank of captain and served at the American Embassy in London. When he returned to New Mexico, he continued his work in publishing and started his political career in the Republican Party. In 1927, Cutting was elected as a senator, a position he held until 1935. Twenty-five years earlier, he had arrived in New Mexico almost certain that he would die there from tuberculosis, but he survived. However, fate once again took an unexpected turn, and he died in a plane crash in Missouri in 1935. Within a week of his death, his Democratic opponent, Dennis Chavez, took his position in the U.S. Senate. Cutting's death held great ramifications for New Mexico's Republican Party; not until 1972 would another Republican from New Mexico be elected to the U.S. Senate.

Grace Thompson Edmister decided to make Albuquerque her home following her recovery from tuberculosis. With a passion for music, she had a dream for Albuquerque; although New Mexico's largest city had many economic and cultural attributes, it did not have a symphony. In October 1932, Edmister founded the Albuquerque Civic Symphony. The orchestra of sixty-one members was composed of teachers, housewives, students and businesspeople. Edmister was the conductor for the symphony when it made its debut at the University of New Mexico on November 13, 1932, with two thousand people in attendance. Edmister was the first woman in America to direct a city symphony, and she held that position until 1941. For the next ten years, Edmister also headed the University of New Mexico's music department. She left Albuquerque in 1942 to pursue other professional interests, but she returned as guest conductor for the symphony's twentieth and twenty-fifth anniversaries. In 1970, she moved back to Albuquerque and remained until her death in 1984 at the age of ninety-three.

William R. Lovelace was a young medical student from Missouri when he contracted tuberculosis. Before he spent his life curing others, Lovelace moved to New Mexico in 1906 in search of a cure for himself. He began his practice at Fort Sumner, and seven years later, he moved to Albuquerque. Lovelace worked alongside other physicians in a group practice, and he embraced the idea of working in a group setting. This type of practice went on to become the business model for the Lovelace Medical Center. Today, Lovelace and its affiliate, the Lovelace Health Plan, are instrumental in providing health care throughout the state of New Mexico.

In 1910, Albert Simms and his wife, Ruth, were living in Arkansas when they were stricken with tuberculosis and decided to move to New Mexico. Three years later, Albert's brother, John, also came down with consumption and followed Albert to a sanatorium in Silver City. Ruth Simms died from the disease, but both brothers recovered and became politicians in the state. After receiving a law degree from the University of New Mexico, Albert opened a practice in Albuquerque. He later became an elected official with the Albuquerque City Council, the Bernalillo County Commission, the New Mexico House of Representatives and the U.S. House of Representatives. During his time in politics, Albert also served on the Republican National Committee. John Simms, who was also a lawyer, served in the New Mexico

Supreme Court, and from 1929 to 1930, he served as chief justice. His son, John Jr., was the governor of New Mexico from 1955 to 1957.

Carrie Wooster came down with tuberculosis in 1910 in her native state of Arkansas. She came to Albuquerque to recover, and her fiancé, Clyde Tingley, soon followed and married her in Albuquerque. When Carrie recovered, the couple decided to make New Mexico a better place as a way to thank the state for their new lives. Clyde rose quickly in the political arena and was elected governor of New Mexico in 1934 and again in 1936. After barely surviving her devastating illness, Carrie Tingley had great empathy for the sick and suffering, especially children. She devoted her life to helping disabled children with polio. In 1937, the Carrie Tingley Hospital opened in Truth or Consequences, New Mexico. It was moved to Albuquerque in 1981, where it continues to promote the health and well-being of children throughout the state today.

While many of the survivors of tuberculosis made their mark on medicine, politics and commerce in Albuquerque, Santa Fe's survivors built the foundation for the city's reputation as a major art center. The city's seven-thousand-foot altitude coupled with its pristine and arid climate brought hundreds of people to Sunmount Sanatorium, which was located in the foothills of the Sangre de Cristo Mountains. The hospital was founded in 1880 by Dr. Frank Mera and his wife, Edna, and it was initially made up of a group of tent houses and small cottages. It was there that the solitude of convalescence awakened a core of creativity in many of the sick patients. The breathtaking landscape that was shaped by volcanic activity millions of years ago, along with the shifting light cast by the sun in the high desert, formed a kaleidoscope of iridescent hues yearning to find artistic expression. The terrain provided a canvas for those indebted to the people and place that gave them a second chance at life.

One person who was instrumental in Santa Fe's transformation into an art mecca was the anthropologist Edgar L. Hewett. He came to Santa Fe from Greeley, Colorado, in 1893 in search of medical help for his wife, Cora Whitford, who suffered from tuberculosis and died from the disease in 1905. One of his many contributions to the state was the founding of the Museum of New Mexico in 1909. Unlike Taos, which also had an art colony, Santa Fe was able to attract major artists from the East because Hewett provided a new state-funded venue in which they could exhibit their work. The first major commercial artist to take advantage of the opportunities provided by the Museum of New Mexico was the Portuguese artist and photographer Carlos Vierra. In the early part of the twentieth century,

Dr. Frank Mera founded Sunmount Sanatorium in 1880, and the hospital opened as a group of tent houses and a small cottage. Prior to the advent of antibiotics, the primary treatment for those suffering from tuberculosis was pristine air, sunshine, low humidity and pollution and living in an environment with a high altitude. *Courtesy of the Palace of the Governors [NMHM/DCA]. No. HP.2012.40.*

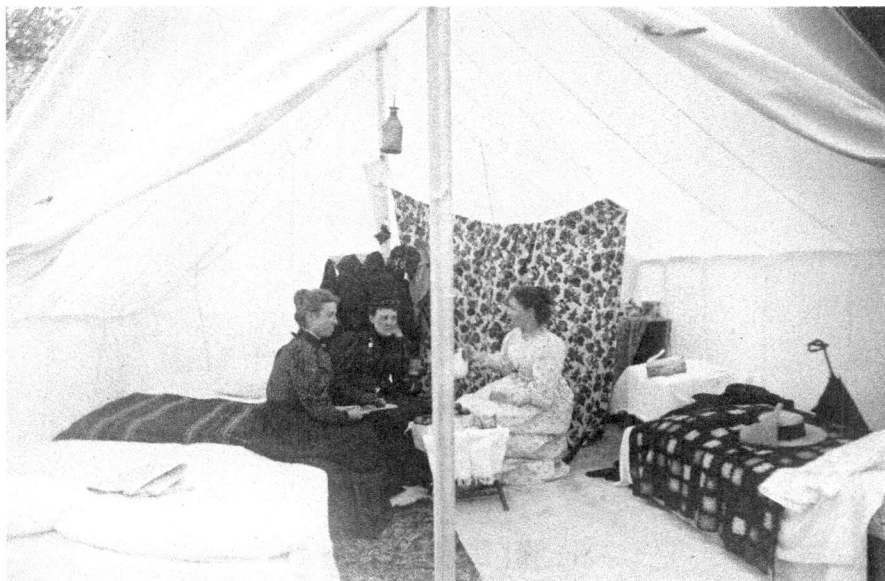

Tuberculosis was the leading cause of death in the United States from the late nineteenth century to 1940. These women were housed in tents while being treated for their lung ailments at Sunmount Sanatorium. *Courtesy of the Palace of the Governors [NMHM/DCA]. No. HP.2014.52.8.*

Vierra moved from New York to Santa Fe seeking a cure for tuberculosis. It was at Sunmount Sanatorium that he met another patient, Brazilian architect John Gaw Meem. The Portuguese language created a bond between the two, which led them to spearhead the Pueblo Revival of Santa Fe architecture. Vierra also helped restore the Palace of the Governors, the oldest capitol building in the United States.

John Gaw Meem was born in Pelotas, Brazil, in 1894, and he immigrated to the United States as a college student. After graduating, he moved to New York to work for his uncle Jim Meem, who was an engineer building the New York City subway. In 1920, John became gravely ill with tuberculosis and moved to Santa Fe for treatment. Known as one of New Mexico's preeminent architects, Meem is credited for his creations of Pueblo Revival–style buildings. During his prolific period, from the 1930s to the 1950s, he designed several buildings, including the Colorado Fine Arts Center in Colorado Springs, the Albuquerque Little Theater and several buildings at the University of New Mexico. In Santa Fe, he designed many structures, including Cristo Rey Church and the county courthouse. A number of his buildings are listed in the National Register of Historic Places.

Carlos Vierra opened an art studio on the Santa Fe Plaza in 1904. A prolific artist and photographer, he collaborated with the School of American Research in the restoration of the Palace of the Governors in 1909. *Courtesy of the Palace of the Governors [NMHM/DCA]. No. 30856.*

Sheldon Parsons was the second artist to arrive in Santa Fe in 1913. A prominent painter in New York, Parsons received commissions from President William McKinley, Vice President Garret Hobart and other well-known politicians of that era. Like Vierra, he came to Santa Fe when he was suffering from tuberculosis. In 1914, he moved into a historic house that was once owned by Padre Gallegos on Washington Avenue. This house soon became a meeting place for the burgeoning artist colony in Santa Fe. Parsons became the first director of the fine arts for the Museum of New Mexico.

Theodore van Soelen came to New Mexico from Minnesota when he was suffering from pneumonia followed by tuberculosis. He met his wife, Virginia

Right: John Gaw Meem was born in Pelotas, Brazil. When he contracted tuberculosis in 1920, while working on the New York City subway, he moved to Santa Fe to convalesce. Meem is one of New Mexico's preeminent architects and is credited for his Pueblo Revival–style buildings. *Courtesy of Nancy Meem Wirth.*

Below: A group photo of artists at La Fonda Hotel in 1925. *Left to right*: Carlos Vierra, Datus Myers, Sheldon Parsons, Theodore Van Soelen, Gerald Cassidy and Will Shuster. With the exception of Datus Myers and Will Shuster, these artists came to New Mexico to be cured from tuberculosis. Shuster suffered from a pulmonary disorder as a result of mustard gas poisoning during World War I. *Photograph by Harmon T. Parkhurst [NMHM/DCA]. No. 020787.*

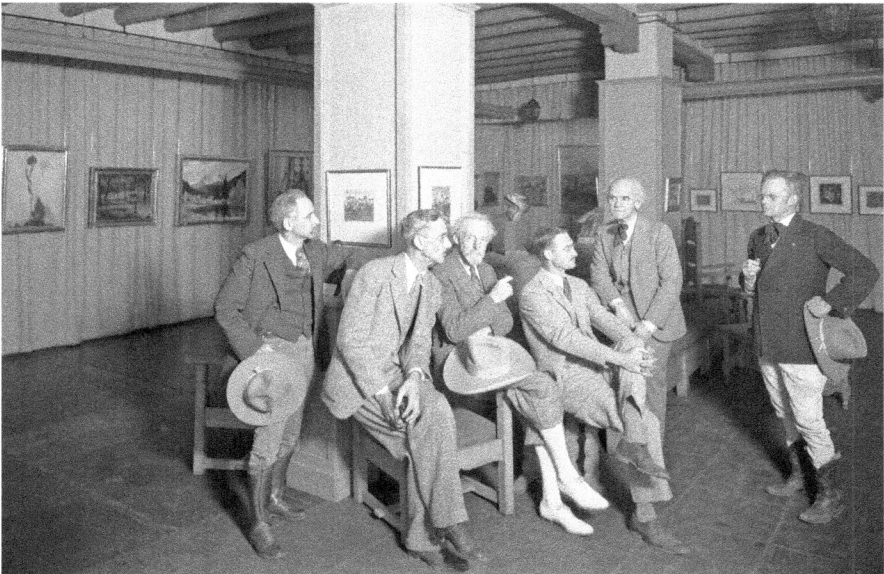

Carr, in Albuquerque in 1921. She was the daughter of a prominent cattle baron. The couple built a house in the village of Tesuque, six miles north of Santa Fe, in 1926. During the Great Depression, he was one of the artists chosen to paint a fresco at the Grant County Courthouse in Silver City, New Mexico, for the Works Progress Administration (WPA).

Gerald Cassidy was born in Covington, Kentucky, in 1869. He pursued an art career in New York, where he became a successful lithographer. Stricken with pneumonia that led to tuberculosis in 1890, he was given six months to live. Cassidy headed west to convalesce at a sanatorium in Albuquerque, where he recovered. In 1912, the year of New Mexico's foundation as a state, Cassidy moved to Santa Fe with his wife, the journalist Ina Sizer. By 1915, the couple was living at the corner of Canyon Road and Acequia Madre Street. In a cruel twist of fate, Cassidy died from the toxic fumes of turpentine and carbon monoxide emitted by a newly installed gas heater in 1934, the year that natural gas heating was introduced to Santa Fe.

RITUALS OF A DIFFERENT KIND

D uring the nineteenth century, New Mexico's most common form of capital punishment was death by hanging. These early executions were made public in the belief that they would deter crime, but these public hangings soon began to resemble a celebratory community event. Businesses would close for the day, and families would dress in their finest clothes and bring picnic lunches to watch criminals as they were hanged. There were vendors that would sell photos of the condemned and promise their customers pieces of the rope after the hanging. The crowds would grow so large that people would take to the rooftops of the surrounding buildings for a better view of the show at the scaffold. By 1835, a new law was enacted to put an end to the spectacle of public hangings, allowing for only law enforcement and dignitaries to witness hangings.

The punishment of death by hanging has its roots in twelfth-century Europe, and it became prevalent in colonial America during the Salem witch trials of 1692. In New Mexico, Spanish colonists routinely hanged Pueblo tribal members who retaliated against their forced servitude. The largest mass execution by hanging in the United States occurred in 1862, when President Abraham Lincoln sanctioned the hanging of thirty-nine Sioux tribal members convicted of murdering white settlers in Mankato, Minnesota.

A surge of hangings followed the gold rush of 1840, as thousands of people ventured through the region, which had little, if any, law enforcement available to provide support for an unruly society. Violence quickly became

This is an image of the hanging of Herman Maestas in Las Vegas, New Mexico, in 1894. Men climbed the fence and wall surrounding the scaffold to get a better view of the condemned man in his final moments. *Courtesy of the Palace of the Governors [NMHM/DCA]. No. 177014.*

the order of the day in the region. In 1837, Governor Albino Perez was decapitated by an angry mob, who removed him from office for raising taxes and for the fact that he was not a native-born New Mexican. His murder went unpunished, as did many crimes during the period in which the region was known as the Wild West.

Another decapitation that drew attention to New Mexico was the bungled execution of outlaw Black Jack Ketchum in 1901. Death by hanging was the mandatory punishment for murderers, but Ketchum's only crime was holding up a railroad train. Legend says that on the morning of his execution, Ketchum told the sheriff, after he ate breakfast, "Let's get this thing over with. I want to get to Hell in time for dinner." Over 150 tickets were issued to witness his death, but the execution took a turn that no one could have ever imagined. As the trapdoor of the scaffold opened, the hangman's noose jolted back, severing Ketchum's head from his body. While his head was still hanging in the noose, Ketchum's lifeless body lay beneath the scaffold. Black Jack Ketchum's hanging is one of the most horrific examples of capital punishment in this country's history.

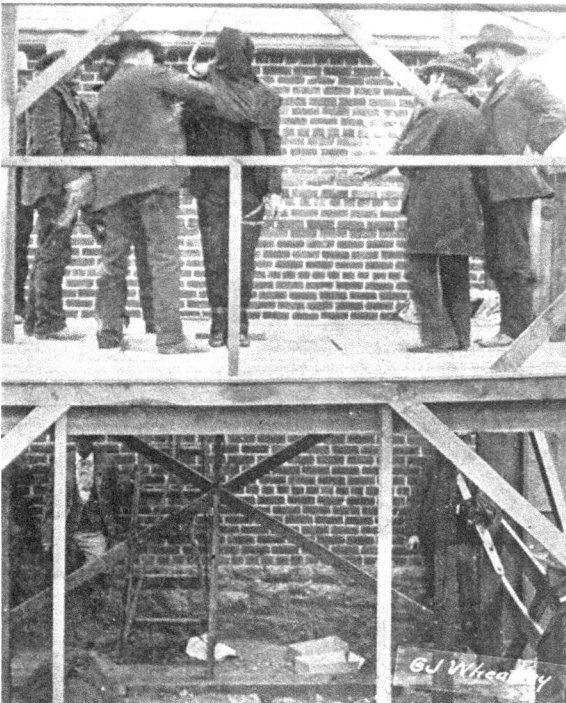

Above: On the day of Black Jack Ketchum's execution, 150 tickets were issued for people to witness his death in a turn of events that no one could have ever imagined. *Courtesy of the Palace of the Governors [NMHM/DCA]. No. 041086.*

Left: Men place a hood on Black Jack Ketchum and secure the noose around his neck minutes before his hanging. *Courtesy of the Palace of the Governors [NMHM/DCA]. No. 128886.*

The headless body of Black Jack Ketchum immediately following his accidental decapitation. His hanging has gone down in history as one of the most horrific executions in the United States. *Courtesy of the Palace of the Governors [NMHM/DCA]. No. 041084.*

Following the American Civil War, criminal justice was sparse; mob vigilantes took the law into their own hands and hanged people without the benefit of a trial. These public executions known as lynchings took place well into the early part of the twentieth century. Many of these hangings were of African Americans in the South and of Native people in the West. With the exception of some of the towns in central New Mexico, there were not many large trees, so lynching victims were hanged from the rooftops of buildings, telephone poles and large billboards.

Assassinations of both the innocent and the guilty were rampant during this era. In 1890, the murder of an aspiring politician in Santa Fe captivated the town with riveting headlines in the daily paper.

Faustín Ortiz, a former deputy sheriff and policeman, and a young man who was beginning to develop some strength in political circles, disappeared very mysteriously on the night of March 1. It was known that he had incurred the displeasure of a number of former associates, many of them

A group of Yaqui tribal members are lynched in a tree in 1905. These types of mob lynchings instilled fear throughout the region. *Courtesy of the Palace of the Governors [NMHM/ DCA]. No. 65377.*

holding office at the time. A $1,000.00 [reward] *has been raised by friends and associates for information leading to his disappearance, including a large reward from the governor.*

The drama, which the media dutifully reported, held the entire comunity in suspense as it continued to unfold.

FOUND DEAD! Faustín Ortiz' body found this afternoon. Found buried in a sandy arroyo. Partly eaten off by animals. Intense excitement throughout the City. Alarm was given, and in 30 minutes 1,000 people were congregating at the spot. Friends of the missing Faustín Ortiz were the first on the scene, and sand was scraped away only sufficiently to permit them to recognize the clothing which Faustín wore when he disappeared so mysteriously on the night of March 1. The mystery is only partially solved. Who murdered him?

The murder of Faustín Ortiz, like so many during that era, went unsolved. The family's only recourse was to remorsefully etch on his tombstone:

En Memoria de Faustín Ortiz que fue a asensinado corbardemente por asesinos conosidos en la Ciudad de Santa Fe el día primero de marzo de año 1890 a los 28 años de edad Rogaremos.

In memory of Faustin Ortiz, who was assassinated by cowards and assassins known in the City of Santa Fe the first day of March 1890 of 28 years of age, Pray for Him.

An assassination south of the border that drew international attention was that of Mexico's Francisco "Pancho" Villa in 1923. As a general in the Mexican Revolution, Villa's infamy was legendary. When he was a teenager, he joined a group of revolutionaries in the mountains, where he became a soldier, and in 1912, he narrowly escaped execution by a firing squad with an eleventh-hour telegram from President Madero. In 1913, he became the governor of Chihuahua, and in 1916, Villa led his troops to the border town of Columbus, New Mexico, where they set the town ablaze, killing nineteen people. President Woodrow Wilson ordered the capture of Villa and set General John Pershing in pursuit of the bandit. Two years later, Pershing and his six thousand troops returned from Mexico empty handed. Villa's reputation caught the attention of Hollywood, and he was brought to the world's stage with film clips of his escapades. But in 1923, Villa's luck ran out when the desperado was gunned down in the southern state of Chihuahua. As he was being driven down a street in Parral, his car was ambushed by eight gunmen. He died instantly from sixteen bullet wounds: two bullets per assassin. Villa was buried in a cemetery in Parral, and three years later, grave robbers desecrated his remains and made off with his head. The body of Pancho Villa was disinterred for a second time in 1976, when it was moved to be reburied at the monument that was built for the revolution in Mexico City.

Death rituals in the military include the custom of riderless horses in funeral processions. This tradition dates back to the fourteenth century, when mourners would lead the deceased person's horse to the burial site and sacrifice it, believing that the animal would follow his master into the afterlife. The first military funeral in America to utilize the riderless horse was that of President George Washington. Traditionally, the horse will follow the funeral caisson, which carries the casket, with the boots reversed in its

The headlines in the *Daily New Mexican* reporting on the murder of Faustín Ortiz. *Courtesy of* La Herencia *Photo Archives.*

saddle's stirrups to represent the fallen leader looking back on his troops for the last time. The tradition of the riderless horse is also featured in military parades to symbolize groups of fallen soldiers.

The funeral train was also a significant ritual that started with a U.S. president. In 1865, the body of President Abraham Lincoln traveled by train from Washington, D.C., to Springfield, Illinois, for its interment. The funeral train also contained the remains of his eleven-year-old son, Willie, who had died three years earlier from typhoid fever. Thousands of people lined the railroad tracks on the route to catch a glimpse of the nation's sixteenth president. Other presidents have been carried to their final resting places on a funeral train; most recently, President George H.W. Bush was carried by a funeral train before his burial in 2018. During the American Civil War, trains were used for the transportation

Left: The tombstone of Faustín Ortiz condemning his assassins in Santa Fe in 1890. *Courtesy of* La Herencia *Photo Archives.*

Below: The body of Francisco "Pancho" Villa hangs out of the passenger door of a 1919 Dodge Roadster in Parral, Mexico, on July 20, 1923. *Courtesy of the Albuquerque Museum. No. PA1977.065.171.*

Death of Villa

A riderless horse was part of the funeral for Doughbell Price in Taos in 1963. *Courtesy of the Palace of the Governors [NMHM/DCA]. No. 029705.*

Bystanders meet a funeral train at the depot in Las Vegas, New Mexico, in 1882. *Courtesy of the Albuquerque Museum. No. PA1978.050.661.*

U.S. soldiers stand beside caskets at a funeral for U.S. servicemen killed in the Columbus Raid in March 1916. *Courtesy of the Albuquerque Museum. No. PA1977.065.152.*

Soldiers load caskets bearing troops killed in the Columbus Raid onto a railroad car in March 1916. *Courtesy of the Albuquerque Museum. No. PA1977.065.153.*

of thousands of soldiers who died far from home. The families of the fallen heroes would also travel by train to reach the battlefield where a loved one had died. When they were able to find the marked graves of their family members, they would often have the body disinterred and taken back home by a train to be buried.

DAY OF THE DEAD

To the modern Mexican, death doesn't have any meaning… To the inhabitant of New York, Paris or London, death is a word that is never uttered because it burns the lips. The Mexican, on the other hand, frequents it, mocks it, caresses it, sleeps with it, celebrates it. It is one of his favorite toys and most permanent lover.
—*Octavio Paz, from* The Labyrinth of Solitude *(1950)*

The indigenous people of Mexico have always had a unique relationship with death. More than three thousand years ago, the ancient civilizations of the Aztecs, Mayans, Totoncas and the Purepecha believed that death completed the cycle of life. The completion of the life-death cycle was seen as both a natural and logical part of existence. Rather than focus on the actual death of a person, these ancient people would concentrate on the journey of their spirit. Although their physical body was no longer viable, a person's soul could travel to another realm, to Mictlan, where the Aztecs believed spirits went for eternity. For pre-Hispanic Mexicans, the concept of good and bad did not exist at the time of death—there was no Heaven nor Hell, nothing to fear. There were no thoughts of final judgment or reincarnation.

When the Spanish conquistadors arrived in the sixteenth century, the concept of death in Mexico evolved into an ordeal of dreaded proportions. European Catholicism introduced Heaven, Hell and Purgatory. Through their forced conversion to Christianity, Mexico's first inhabitants were taught to fear death—to live virtuously or face eternal damnation! The Spanish

Mexico has always maintained a unique relationship with death. *Illustration by Jose Guadalupe Posada. Courtesy of the Library of Congress.*

clergy brought their medieval prophecies about the end of the world and images of the corpses of sinners being devoured by worms as they entered the gates of Hell with them. But those prophesies were the least of the Native Mexicans' problems; the actual slaughter and torture inflicted on the Natives proved to be the most frightening European innovation, as did the alien diseases, like smallpox, that decimated the Native population.

By the 1800s, a tide of nationalism swept through Mexico, and the underpinning of European domination began to wane. After centuries of exploitation, the indigenous Mexican people began to reclaim their identities and early belief systems, which included the belief that death—not the actual moment of one's demise but rather the spiritual journey after—was not to be feared. Paintings of Death as a jovial skeleton began to appear, and images of skulls and skeletons started to decorate temple walls. Skeleton puppets, toys and skulls made from sugar became popular items at street markets. A symbiotic relationship had begun to build between November 2 (All Soul's Day on the Catholic calendar) and Día de los Muertos (the Day of the Dead for the Indigenous). The holiday is centered on the days that the spirits of passed family members can come back to their burial place and to the homes where they once lived to be with their loved ones. The living painstakingly prepare funeral altars at home with candles, decorative flowers and the favorite foods of the deceased. Once that task is completed, they go to the cemetery, sweep the gravesite and bring food and drink to sing songs for the visiting spirits. There are no tears or prayers, for the families have already shared those emotions at the actual funeral; this is a joyous event for the families and the eternal spirits of their loved ones.

The *calavera* has become synonymous with Mexico's Day of the Dead tradition. The English translation of *calavera* is skull, but in Mexico, the term has come to embrace the entire skeleton as a representation of the dead. No one popularized the *calavera* more in Mexico than Jose Guadalupe Posada. Although he did not invent the art form of the *calavera*, his skeleton illustrations popularized the ancient motifs found in the prehistoric art of Mexico's Indigenous people. He used caricatures of cheerful skeletons to imitate life while simultaneously providing a commentary on its absurdities—Posada's art breathed life into death.

Jose Guadalupe Posada was born in 1852 in the countryside of Aguascalientes, and he died in Mexico City in 1913. During his lifetime, he created more than fifteen thousand illustrations. His illustrations were later reproduced during the heyday of the Penny Press in Mexico, whose mission was to enlighten, engage and enrage. Not all of his prints were of the *calavera*, but those are the ones that people identify with on the Day of

The *calavera* has become synonymous with Mexico's Day of the Dead tradition. *Illustration by Jose Guadalupe Posada. Courtesy of the Library of Congress.*

The illustrations by Jose Guadalupe Posada of the *calavera* gave the dead an opportunity to come back to life. *Illustration by Jose Guadalupe Posada. Courtesy of the Library of Congress.*

the Dead. More than any other artist, Jose Guadalupe Posada reminded us that, in death, all enjoy equality. Posada's work inspired Diego Rivera, Mexico's most widely known artist of the twentieth century. As a small boy, Rivera would go to the print shop where Posada worked to watch him draw. In 1947, Rivera paid homage to Posada by including his image, along with his own as a small boy, in one of his best-known murals, *Sueño de una tarde dominical en la Alameda Centra*, which was featured at the Hotel del Prado in Mexico City until the earthquake of 1985. Fortunately, the mural was not destroyed and now resides in a museum created for the work that is called Museo Mural Diego Rivera.

The festivities for Día de los Muertos in Mexico usually start during the last week of October and lead up to the November 2 holiday. Throughout small towns and big cities, vendors lay out the traditional products needed for the *ofrendas* (altars)—flowers, incense, candles, saints and crosses—that will be accompanied by photos of the dead and bits of memorabilia associated with them. Bakeries fire up their ovens to make massive amounts of the traditional "bread of the dead," which is elaborately decorated with skull images. Many of the other foods prepared for the altars and gravesites include corn tamales, mole, pumpkin and hot chocolate. Some altars include beer and tequila in remembrance of the dearly departed who indulged in drink. Paper and cardboard skeletons, and those made with electronic lights, are sold at markets as home decorations. After gathering at the altar for the start of the celebration, families travel to the cemetery, where they share stories and memories of their dearly beloved, departed family members. Parents present toys and candy-shaped skulls to their children to reinforce the idea that death is not to be feared but celebrated in the circle of life.

Ironically, while New Mexico was a part of Mexico from 1821 to 1846, the tradition of Día de los Muertos did not become popular in the state until the latter part of the twentieth century. For two hundred years, New Mexico was a part of Spain, and most Hispanics identified as being of Spanish descent, in spite of the fact that the state shared more cultural characteristics with Mexico. Following the end of the Mexican Revolution in 1920, the *corridos* (folk ballads) of Mexico became very popular in New Mexico. Many of these songs, like "*Un Puño de Tierra*" (A Fistful of Dirt), pertained to death. Here are some of the lyrics to "*Puño de Tierra*" in Spanish and English:

> *Vagando voy por la vida*
> *Nomás recoriendo el mundo*
> *Si quieren que se diga*
> *Yo soy un alma sin dueño*
> *A mí no me importa nada*
> *Pa' mí la vida es un sueño*
>
> *Yo tomo cuando yo querio*
> *No, soy muy sincero.*
> *Y soy como las gaviotas*
> *Volando de puerto en puerto*
> *Yo sé que la vida es corta*
> *Al fin que también la debo*
>
> *El día que me muera*
> *No voy a llevarme me nada*
> *Hay darle gusto al gusto*
> *La vida pronto se acaba*
> *Lo que pasó en este mundo*
> *Nomás el recuerdo queda*
> *Ya muerto voy a llevarme*
> *Nomás un puño de tierra*

No more going around the world
If you want me to tell you
I am a soul without an owner
I don't care about anything
For life is a dream

I drink when I want
I do not lie, I am very sincere
And I'm like the seagulls
Flying from port to port
I know that life is short
At last I owe it

The day I die
I'm not going to take anything
There is taste to taste
Life is soon over
What happened in this world
No more memory is left
Already dead I will take me
Only a fist of earth

Slowly, the Mexican concept of death crept into New Mexico's collective psyche, and several of those Mexican ballads continue to fill the airways and are sung at funerals. By the 1980s, the Mexican community in New Mexico had grown significantly with Mexico's cultural characteristics becoming mainstream. Today, large celebrations of Día de los Muertos are held on November 2 in the state and in major Hispanic communities throughout the Southwest. Like their counterparts in Mexico, New Mexican families create altars at home to welcome the returning spirits. Graves are cleaned and prepared for the presentation of favorite foods and beverages to their deceased loved ones. Some family members gather for dusk-to-dawn vigils in the hopes of being reunited with their ancestors in the circle of life celebration.

In New Mexico, ceremonies are primarily confined to the graveyard, but in Mexico, for many weeks leading up to the celebration, images of *calaveras* are ubiquitous, finding their way into storefront windows and school curriculums. Another Mexican tradition is to encourage people to "think" for the dead by writing humorous verses that convey life's inevitable passage.

An offering is prepared for the Feast Day of the Dead at Isleta Pueblo on November 2. In Pueblo tradition, it is said that if the deceased lived a good life, they only need a little food for their journey to the spirit world. However, if the opposite was true, they need more food for their journey. *Photograph by Charles F. Lummis. Courtesy of the Palace of the Governors [NMHM/ DCA]. No. 136371.*

In New Mexico, the celebration of Día de los Muertos is usually held at the cemetery. This image shows traditional food offerings at the gravesite. *Photograph by Nancy Warren Hunter. Courtesy of the Palace of the Governors [NMHM/DCA]. No. HP.2003.29.40.*

A timeless masterpiece of this regional genre was written by the man who popularized Día de los Muertos. In an illustration by Jose Guadalupe Posada, two skeletons are languishing in purgatory, contemplating the arrival of death, when one says to the other, "*Hoy por ti, y mañana para mi,*" which translates to, "Today for you and tomorrow for me."

BIBILIOGRPAPHY

Introduction

The Bosque Redondo Memorial. "Remembering Their Past, Celebrating Their Future." www.bosqueredondomemorial.com.

Brunson-Hadley, Judy L., and Douglas R. Mitchell, ed. *Ancient Burial Practices in the American Southwest*. Albuquerque: University of New Mexico Press, 2001.

Roach, Mary. *Stiff: The Curious Lives of Human Cadavers*. New York: Norton, 2003.

Weiss, Bari. "A Dress Rehearsal for Our Deaths." *New York Times*, September 17, 2018.

Wikipedia. "Dark Tourism." www.wikipedia.org.

Chapter One

Canadian Museum of History. "Mumification." www.historymuseum.ca.

Clark, Liesl. "Mummies 101." PBS. www.pbs.org.

Conservapedia. "Diagoras of Melos." www.conservapedia.com.

German, Dr. Senta. "The Cradle of Civilization." Khan Academy. www.khanacademy.org.

Kerrigan, Michael. *The History of Death*. Guilford, CT: Lyons Press, 2007.

Mingren, Wu. "Zoroastrian Towers of Silence: Where the Dead Are Left to the Vultures." Ancient Origins. www.ancient-origins.net.

Stenudd, Stefan. "Cosmos of the Ancients." Philosophers. www.stenudd.com.

Torres, Jair Cabrera. "At a Sprawling Shrine to Shiva, Nepal's Hindus Help the Dead on Their Way." Religion News Service. www.religionnews.com.

Chapter Two

Cordova, Benito G. "Descansos: New Mexico's Highway Markers to Heaven." *La Herencia*, 1994.

Dunnington, Jacqueline. "The Cross: A Universal Symbol." *La Herencia*, 2000.

Johnson, Chandra. "Leyendes: Descansos Mark Honored New Mexican Tradition." Taos News. www.taosnews.com.

Pacheco, Ana. "Angelo." *La Herencia*, 1998.

Roadside America. "Descansos: Highway Fatality Memorials." www.roadsideamerica.com.

Chapter Three

Armenta, Steve. "The Ghost of the PERA Building." *La Herencia*, 1997.

De Chaparro, Martina Will. *Death and Dying in New Mexico*. Albuquerque: University of New Mexico Press, 2007.

Delgado, Casimira. "El Velorio." *La Herencia*, 1995.

Funeral Guide. "Death Around the World: Native American Beliefs." www.funeralzone.com.

Kerrigan, Michael. *The History of Death*. Guilford, CT: Lyons Press, 2007.

Mondragon, Roberto, and Georgia Roygal. "Velorios Chilorios." *La Herencia*, 1995.

Moya, Emma. "Getting the Word Out: A Matter of Life and Death." *La Herencia*, 1995.

Native American Netroots. "1467 Diary." www.nativeamericannetroots.net.

Pacheco, Ana. *A History of Spirituality in Santa Fe: The City of Holy Faith*. Charleston, SC: The History Press, 2016.

Padilla, Pat. "Local Men's Organizations Promote Cultural Preservation." *La Herencia*, 1994.

Roach, Mary. *Stiff: The Curious Lives of Human Cadavers*. New York: Norton, 2003.

Vigil, Maurilio, E. "Hispanos and the Santa Fe Trail." *La Herencia*, 2004

Chapter Four

Armijo, Abel. Interview with the author on the Cristo Rey Cemetery, April 2019.

Arrey, Tommy. Interview with the author on the Cristo Rey Cemetery, April 2019.

Bove, Phillip. Interview with the author on the Cristo Rey Cemetery, April 2019.

Brunson-Hadley, Judy L., and Douglas R. Mitchell, ed. *Ancient Burial Practices in the American Southwest*. Albuquerque: University of New Mexico Press, 2001.

Cordova, Kathryn M. *¡Concha! Concha Ortiz y Pino, Matriarch of a 300-Year-Old New Mexico Legacy*. Santa Fe, NM: Gran Via, 2006.

Cruz, Patricio A. "Los Penitentes." *La Herencia*, 2005.

De Chaparro, Martina Will. *Death and Dying in New Mexico*. Albuquerque: University of New Mexico Press, 2007.

De Chaparro, Martina Will, and Miruna Achim. *Death and Dying in Colonial Spanish America*. Tucson: University of Arizona Press, 2011.

DuBois, Ramona. "La Morada." *La Herencia*, 1997.

Dunnington, Jacqueline. "Here Lies New Mexico." *La Herencia*, 2007.

Martinez, Paul H. "Angelitos." *La Herencia*, 2009.

Miera, Rudy J. "La Noche Buena y Nuestros Antepasodos." *La Herencia*, 1996.

Ortiz-Jacquez, Michele. "Indian Life Through the Eye of John S. Candelario." *La Herencia*, 2000. The Santa Fe National Cemetery Visitors Guide. Santa Fe, NM.

———. "John Candelario, Photographer Extraordinaire." *La Herencia*, 2000.

Pacheco, Ana. *A History of Spirituality in Santa Fe: The City of Holy Faith*. Charleston, SC: The History Press, 2016.

Ribera-Ortega, Pedro. "Processions: A March of Faith." *La Herencia*, 1995.

Rodriguez, Pete. Interview with the author on the Cristo Rey Cemetery, April 2019.

Romero, Edward. "Generations of Faith." *La Herencia*, 2007.

Taylor, J. Paul. "My Pickled Grandfather." *La Herencia*, 2007.

Trujillo, Manuel. Interview with the author on the Cristo Rey Cemetery, April 2019.

Valdez, Carlos. Interview with the author on the Cristo Rey Cemetery, April 2019.

Chapter Five

Baca-Vaughn, Guadalupe. "Padre Martinez." *La Herencia*, 1997.

Contreras, Russel. "Proposal Seeks Memorial for US Civil War Site in New Mexico." *Albuquerque Journal*. www.abqjournal.com.

Dunnington, Jacqueline. "Here Lies New Mexico." *La Herencia*, 2007.

Encyclopedia Britannica. "Kit Carson." www.britannica.com.

Flint, Richard, and Shirley Cushing. "Lucien Maxwell." New Mexico History. www.newmexicohistory.org.

Fox New Mexico. "Map of Veterans Memorials." www.krqe.com.

Gutierrez, Ezekiel. "Forgotten Cemeteries in Albuquerque." *La Herencia*, 2005.

History. "Billy the Kid Is Shot to Death." www.history.com.

Legends of America. "The Largest Land Grant in US History—Maxwell Land Grant." www.legendsofamerica.com.

————. "Navajo Long Walk to the Bosque Redondo." www.legendsofamerica. com.

Leven, Carrie. "Sign #2 Kiowa Trail and Sentinel Peak." Questa History Trail. www.questatrail.org.

New Mexico Energy, Minerals and Natural Resources Department. "Welcome to Smokey Bear State Park!" www.emnrd.state.nm.us.

Oswald, Mark. "Legislation Calls for Plans for New Civil War Memorial." *Albuquerque Journal*. www.abqjournal.com.

Pacheco, Ana. *Early Santa Fe*. Charleston, SC: Arcadia Publishing, 2017.

————. *Legendary Locals of Santa Fe*. Charleston, SC: Arcadia Publishing, 2013.

Peña, Abe M. "Truth Comes for the Archbishop." *La Herencia*, 2000.

Peoples of the Mesa Verde Region. "The Long Walk." www.crowcanyon.org.

Rivera, Lydia. "Alejandrito: Santa Fe's Angel of Death." *La Herencia*, 1994.

Stamatov, Suzanne. "D.H. Lawrence." New Mexico History. www. newmexicohistory.org.

U.S. Forest Service. "The Story of Smokey Bear." www.fs.fed.us.

Vigil, Maurilio E. "La Tules: A Santa Fe Legend." *La Herencia*, winter 2007.

Chapter Six

Cordova, Kathryn M. *¡Concha! Concha Ortiz y Pino, Matriarch of a 300-Year-Old New Mexico Legacy*. Santa Fe, NM: Gran Via, 2004.

Cruz, Patricio, A. "Los Penitentes." *La Herencia*, 2005.

De Chaparro, Martina Will. *Death and Dying in New Mexico*. Albuquerque: University of New Mexico Press, 2007.

Lopez, Walter K. "Socorro's Ethnic Diversity." *La Herencia*, 2001.

Meier, Allison. "The Lost Ritual of Photographing the Dead." Hyperallergic. www.hyperallergic.com.

Pacheco, Ana. *A History of Spirituality in Santa Fe: The City of Holy Faith*. Charleston, SC: The History Press, 2016.

Rivera, Lydia. "La Carreta de la Muerte." *La Herencia*, spring 1997.

Chapter Seven

Garcia, Nasario, and Richard McCord. *Albuquerque Feliz Cumpleaños: Three Centuries to Remember*. Santa Fe, NM: Gran Via, 2003.

Gonzalez, Herminia C. "Influenza Hits Las Vegas with Epidemic Proportions." *La Herencia*, 1996.

Goodman, Alan H., and Debra L. Martin. "Health Conditions Before Columbus: Paleopathology of Native North Americans." National Center for Biotechnology Information. www.ncbi.nlm.nih.gov.

Nunn, Nathan, and Nancy Qian. "The Columbian Exchange: A History of Disease, Food, and Ideas." Northwestern University. www.kellogg. northwestern.edu.

Pascual, Katrina. "Diseases Brought by European Colonists Crippled Population of Native Americans in the 17th Century." Tech Times. www. techtimes.com.

Chapter Eight

De Chaparro, Martina Will. *Death and Dying in New Mexico*. Albuquerque: University of New Mexico Press, 2007.

Gilbreat, West. *Death on the Gallows: The Story of Legal Hanging in New Mexico 1847–1923*. Silver City, NM: High-Lonesome Books, 2002.

History. "Pancho Villa Attacks Columbus, New Mexico." www.history.com.

Pacheco, Ana. "The Murder of Faustín Ortiz." *La Herencia*, 2006.

Politibrew. "The Riderless Horse: Empty Boots Reversed in the Stirrups." www.politibrew.com.

Torrez, Robert. "Hangings and Lynchings in New Mexico." New Mexico History. www.newmexicohistory.org.

Weiser, Kathy. "Train Robber—Black Jack Ketchum." Legends of America. www.legendsofamerica.com.

Chapter Nine

Moya, Emma. "Songs of the Revolution." *La Herencia*, 1996.

Tyler, Ron, ed. *Posada's Mexico*. Edited by the Library of Congress. Washington, D.C., 1979.

Younis, Rita. "Día de los Muertos." *La Herencia*, 1997.

INDEX

ABOUT THE AUTHOR

Photograph by Linda Carfegno.

This is the fifth book Ana Pacheco has written for Arcadia and The History Press and the tenth book about New Mexico's history in which she is listed as either the author or editor. Pacheco was the city historian of Santa Fe from 2015 to 2017. She was also the founding publisher and editor of *La Herencia*, a quarterly magazine on New Mexico history that was published from 1994 to 2009. From 2007 to September 2013, Pacheco wrote the weekly column "A Wonderful Life" for the *Santa Fe New Mexican*, which documented the oral histories of the elder community. In 2010, she published the official magazine for Santa Fe's quadricentennial.

Pacheco is the daughter of Jesús Pacheco and Natalie Ortiz. Her Ortiz ancestors settled in Santa Fe in 1692. Her mother, Natalie Ortiz, was a descendant of Diego de Vargas, who led the resettlement of Santa Fe after the Pueblo Revolt of 1692. Don Gaspar Avenue is named after Ana's great-great-grandfather Don Gaspar Ortiz. The Ortiz Room at the Santa Fe Hilton Hotel and Ortiz Street located in the plaza area are named in honor of her grandfather several times removed Nicolás Ortiz. Her Pacheco ancestors arrived in Santa Cruz, New Mexico, in 1739 and moved to Santa Fe in the late 1800s. The busy thoroughfare Pacheco Street is named after Ana's great-grandfather Jose de la Cruz Pacheco.

In 1976, Pacheco moved to New York, where she began her publishing career. She was a freelance writer and held various positions with entertainment, Hispanic and financial service publications as an advertising and international marketing executive. Pacheco returned to Santa Fe in 1992 and served on the Board of Directors for the National Hispanic Cultural Center for the State of New Mexico for seven years. She hosted a weekly Hispanic radio show for Citadel Communications for three years and served on the Wells Fargo Community Advisory Board and Santa Fe Fiesta Foundation Board for several years.

Pacheco became a Paul Harris Fellow of the Rotary Foundation of Rotary International in 2010. The award was in appreciation of tangible and significant assistance given for the furtherance of better understanding and friendly relations among people of the world. In 2009, Pacheco received a Certificate of Appreciation from Santa Fe County for her work with the city's Hispanic and elderly communities. She received the 2008 Heritage Preservation Award from the City of Santa Fe for excellence in community traditions for her work with *La Herencia*. Pacheco is a 2007 recipient of the New Mexico Community Foundation Luminaria award for her leadership and contributions to the state of New Mexico. In 2006, she was awarded two national awards by the National Association of Press Women. She is also a 2004 recipient of the Governor's Award for outstanding women of New Mexico and an award from PEN New Mexico for her efforts to preserve Hispanic culture, history and language. PEN New Mexico is the state's affiliate of the largest international professional association of writers, editors and translators. For more information, visit www.historyinsantafe.com or Threads of Santa Fe History on YouTube.

www.ingramcontent.com/pod-product-compliance
Lightning Source LLC
Chambersburg PA
CBHW040135270326
41927CB00019B/3399